For the child who "won't color inside the lines" . . .

Challenging children need special treatment—because they are special. Bright, creative, curious, or just exceptionally independent, they can sometimes make things tough for parents and teachers—but their unique qualities can also bring joyful and exciting rewards if properly nurtured.

The Challenging Child offers parents wise, practical advice about dealing with nonconforming children—in ways that maintain discipline and encourage maturity, but allow the special spirit of the challenging child to flourish. Learn how to . . .

- identify the challenging child
- deal with extroverted or introverted children
- diffuse conflict through discipline
- find the right school for your child
- help your child overcome shyness

And more

THE CHALLENGING CHILD

THE CHALLENGING CHILD

Mitch Golant, Ph.D.,
and
Donna G. Corwin

BERKLEY BOOKS, NEW YORK

THE CHALLENGING CHILD

A Berkley Book / published by arrangement with
the authors

PRINTING HISTORY
Berkley trade paperback edition / September 1995

ISBN: 0-425-14953-6

BERKLEY®
Berkley Books are published by The Berkley Publishing Group,
200 Madison Avenue, New York, New York 10016.
BERKLEY and the "B" design
are trademarks belonging to Berkley Publishing Corporation.

PRINTED IN THE UNITED STATES OF AMERICA

10 9 8 7 6 5 4 3

For my mother, who understood the challenges . . .

—Mitch Golant

To my precious daughter, Alexandra, who challenges me every day to be a better parent.

—Donna Corwin

ACKNOWLEDGMENTS

This book would not have been possible without the trust and confidence that so many children and their families have given to me for more than twenty years. I am forever grateful for what we have shared together.

There are many others who have taught me so much. First, my children, Cherie and Aimee, have given me the opportunity to learn in an immediate and personal way how to maintain love and closeness in the face of adversity and challenges.

Most important, I am grateful to my wife, Susan Golant, who is my deepest soul mate, and whose love makes all the challenges so much sweeter.

I am, of course, indebted to innumerable colleagues and friends whose insights and ideas have helped clarify my own perspective. Specifically, I am grateful to Dr. Anne Panofsky, Dr. Michael Braun, Dr. Marion Schulman, and Susan Levine, MSW, for all their efforts and timely insights. And, to Bob

Tabian, my agent, whose advice and clarity of purpose I deeply respect.

Finally, I'd like to thank Donna Corwin, my coauthor, whose energy and passion for this project, and her willingness to share so many of her challenges helped *The Challenging Child* come alive!

—M.G.

Thank you to my husband, Stan, who encourages my work with his constant support, love, and brilliant editorial eye.

Thank you to Hillary Cige, our editor.

To Terri, my lifelong friend, who has always been there to listen, but never to judge.

To Shirley, my parental mirror, who shares her challenges, her insights, and her friendship.

To Ann Benya, who inspired me to buy a computer. Thanks for the great pages.

To Cassie Goddard, for her assistance.

And a special thank-you to my coauthor, Mitch Golant, whose profound sensitivities and professional insight into challenging children and their parents form the foundation for our book.

—D.C.

CONTENTS

CONTENTS

THE
CHALLENGING CHILD

INTRODUCTION

Alexandra has never been your "primary color kind of kid." If the teacher told the class to draw trees, green would not be the number-one color choice on her list. She would much prefer magenta and yellow with blue stripes.

If you told Alexandra, "Honey, trees are supposed to be green," she would look at you as if you had lost your mind. "Well, I know that!" she'd retort. "But my trees aren't." So there. So that's Alex.

Right from the beginning, I felt her stirring deep inside my womb. She kicked with the intensity of a black belt in karate. Then, she slept shorter, cried louder, giggled longer, and played harder than other babies.

When other babies were eating baby food, she wanted chopped-up chicken. When toddlers were sitting quietly listening to Raffi music, Alexandra wanted to climb the rafters and swing from the chandeliers.

People said she was difficult. But she didn't bite or hit. She wasn't mean or aggressive toward other children. Alexandra is just different. She marches to the beat of her own drum, but her curiosity and differences don't necessarily make her difficult—they make her **challenging.**

Most people will know they have a challenging child very early on. You think your child will outgrow these behaviors; once your toddler becomes a preschooler, socialization will surely calm him down. But in nursery school, your angel refuses to take a nap. When the teacher is reading, your child wants to play blocks. When all the children are drawing dogs, your darling prefers to draw cats. But again, you think this is only a silly phase.

So off to school your little one goes, and now it's the big time. No more indulgence. The challenger meets the challenging. After a few weeks, Mrs. Kindergarten Teacher complains that your child will not line up with the other children when asked. She seems preoccupied and sometimes defiant. She is bored or perhaps interested in a completely different agenda than the teacher has planned. Are you beginning to see a pattern here? Challenging children can be different, unique, socially immature, hyperactive, gifted, or merely high-spirited and precocious. But more often than not, they are not easygoing and compliant. Challengers are high-maintenance children.

The most damaging thing to do is to label a challenging child "bad." These labels immediately brand a child, and brands can damage fragile self-esteem. A parent often becomes impatient with a challenging child, and doesn't usually have the skills to deal with his or her complexities. If you have a challenger, you may see your relationship start to erode when you find yourself spending so much time on discipline and special attention that you fail to enjoy and appreciate any of your child's unique qualities.

Our book will help you identify the traits of a challenger, build stronger support for parents and children, and use positive programs that nurture self-esteem. We understand how frustrating challenging children can be, and we offer concrete solutions that will alter difficult behavior problems, create a relationship with your child's school, and help you help your child in his everyday interactions with teachers, friends, and relatives.

In *The Challenging Child* you will also gain an understanding of your role as a parent and how your attitudes impact your child. Our book addresses more than the child's behavior; it also looks at the parents' behavior within the family structure. Our aim is to not only help you understand and manage your challenging child, but to assist you in better understanding your own temperament, unspoken cues, family interactions, role modeling, and parental behaviors toward your challenger.

A healthy and supportive family can only be attained when you are willing to be flexible and change your attitudes toward your child. A challenger can become the bright spot, not the thorn, in a family's lives.

A psychologist once told me that my daughter may be hard to handle now, strong-willed, defiant, and high-spirited, but as an adult she'd be magnificent. He assured me that all of the characteristics that challenge *me* now would serve *her* wonderfully as an adult. And of course, our role as parents is to raise and guide our children to become happy, self-sufficient adults.

If you are a parent with an active challenger, the most valuable tool we can give you in our book is to learn when to "let it go" and when to "hold on," so that your challenger will have every opportunity to succeed.

The Challenging Child— Not Easy to Define

NOT EASY TO DEFINE

Children are wonderful. They can be warm, loving, amusing, contrary, exhausting, interesting—and **challenging.**

Challenging children can possess all of the above traits and often all at the same time; they can really wear you out. Just when you think life is relatively quiet and under control, something happens with a challenger, and you wonder if your family life will ever be calm.

A challenger is never satisfied. He wants attention constantly. He will whine, plead, and cajole until he gets his way. Unlike other kids, who know when to stop, a challenger will keep at you until you are "worn down."

One little girl kept pushing her mother away every time she went to kiss her. Then, as soon as she walked away, the little girl begged for a kiss.

Many challengers have a spirit that ignites wherever they go. One mother with a challenging eight-year-old confessed, "People have strong positive or negative feelings toward my daughter. She can bring out the best in others and the worst. If she's around a controlling person, then watch out—sparks fly. She locked horns so badly with one teacher at school, I thought the battle of wills would never end. But the following year, her new teacher thought her high spirit and curiosity were delightful. I give up!''

We're asking you not to give up because there is a way to understand your child, help him, and help yourself in the process. Defining a challenger is not an easy task. Some people—teachers, parents, peers—welcome challengers because they understand and nurture their unique personalities. Others see challengers as difficult, unruly, and defiant.

Too often you may define your child by how others view him. Too often a child is put into good and bad categories with nothing in between. "Difficult" has a negative connotation. You have to be careful how you imprint your child. A child hears and feels more than we realize. His self-esteem is shaped by others' labels of him.

BOUNDARIES AND LIMITS

The underlying theme that defines challenging traits is how a child responds to boundaries—both in terms of those he sets for himself, and the ones we set for him.

The issue with a challenger is often the struggle to know where his space ends and yours begins. In social relationships, what a child thinks is his space often invades the space of others. A challenger wants his own way and has trouble seeing another person's point of view. He thinks the way he sees the world is the way we all do.

Boundaries are threatening to a challenger because he feels anxious when a boundary is set. The typical attitude is, "Go ahead. Give me a boundary. Watch me push, negotiate, and be defiant until I get my way." Because of the very nature of these children and their inabilities to contain their emotions, boundaries represent giant walls. Internally they don't believe that they can be confined behind these walls—thus, anxiety is produced.

That is why when we talk about setting limits, we are really talking about limits based on who your child is, not the limits some other parent places on their child. If you look at your best friend's child and see "Miss Well-Behaved," you might make the mistake of implementing the parenting methods established for your friend's child rather than utilizing the limits appropriate for your challenger.

For example, "Miss Well-Behaved" can sit for hours at a restaurant without so much as a peep. "Miss Challenger," on the other hand, has been active and unhappy sitting in a restaurant since she was an infant. If you tell your challenger, "Either you sit for two hours quietly in a restaurant like 'Miss Well-Behaved' or you get punished," this is inappropriate for your child.

In order to set reasonable boundaries for your child, it is important that you have a clear understanding of challenging traits and how each one impacts your attempt to establish limits.

Although every child is unique, there are some defining traits of challengers that most parents will recognize. By defining these traits, we are trying to reassure you that you are dealing with a normal child, with complex needs that may demand a lot of you. It *is* more work to parent a challenger, and chances are you will be working at it for a long time. But with consistent positive reinforcers, a challenger can blossom into a delightful, exciting, vibrant adult. These traits will not apply across the board for every challenger, but more than likely each child will have at least five of them to varying degrees. All of the challenging traits tend to overlap. They have a domino effect; one trait can impact another.

- Pushers and pullers
- Escalators
- Negotiators
- Curiosity seekers
- Competitive
- Easily frustrated
- Strong-willed
- Energetic
- Impatient and not easily satisfied

PUSHERS AND PULLERS

Push, pull, push, pull! This is a familiar song to a challenger. He will push an issue to the edge—to the point that you feel you are going to lose it—and then pull back, waiting for someone to throw him a lifeline.

Challengers respond particularly to authority figures—the rule-makers—like parents and teachers. Traditionally, the very people whom challengers push up against are the same people whom challengers rely on to set boundaries for them.

A youngster who pushes is often anxious inside—anxious to please, anxious to succeed, anxious to be the best. He thinks that if he sets a goal, he *must* accomplish it. This pressure adds to his anxiety. A pusher thinks that if he accomplishes his goal and gets what he wants, the anxiety will diminish. In actuality, it intensifies because he has to keep on winning. So the cycle continues until someone helps him find another route.

A child who consistently pushes, often struggles to feel good about himself. He comes off as having a lot of bravado, but usually this just masks his insecurity. Underneath, a challenger has the need to feel in control. This need for control permeates all aspects of his life. Control helps challengers feel safe; yet, sometimes the need to control pushes others away. A challenger needs to be taught alternate ways of attaining his goals.

In conversations about a future trip to Disneyland, six-year-old Alex's mother tried to talk him out of riding the Matterhorn because she knew he was fearful of fast rides. But he pushed her until she said okay. He bragged about the impending ride during the coming months. He told his friends that he was not afraid and that he was going to ride it ten times. He was even critical of friends who voiced some fear of the roller coaster ride. When Alex finally went to Disneyland and the moment came for him to ride the Matterhorn, he became hysterical. At that point, his mom tried to talk him into getting on the ride, convinced he really wanted to do it. But that didn't work. Then she made matters worse by saying, "Look at all the littler kids going on the ride." His mom finally backed off and let Alex watch the other kids ride the Matterhorn. His friends teased him, which only made Alex feel worse about himself. But his bragging had boxed him into a corner.

Alex, like many pushers, is really just a frightened little boy in "cocky kids' clothing." His bravado helped cover his anxiety. But when the moment of truth came, his insecurity overwhelmed his bravado.

There are many concrete ways to help pushers pull back.

Parent Plan

- Pushers need boundaries and limits. These parameters help the pusher feel like he is safe. He may fight against the limits you impose, but he'll be the happier for them.
- It is vital to support your child's feelings. Alex's mom could have said, "I'm glad you recognize that ride was so scary. Let's talk about it next time. Lots of people are frightened by fast rides. You're not alone. . . ."
- Pushers need a lot of convincing. They have to be told things many times before you see a change in their behavior.
- Be consistent and persistent.

ESCALATORS

Seven-year-old Jessica was tired and cranky. Lynn asked her nicely to please put her toys away. Jessica said, "I'm too tired." Lynn insisted. Suddenly, Jessica started whining and screaming. Lynn told her to be quiet. She cried louder. Within 10 minutes, from Lynn's simple request to have her daughter put her toys away, Jessica was in a complete tantrum. She was screaming, crying, and whining.

Lynn was in a sweat. What happened? How did a simple request become an all-out war?

Such rapid escalation of emotion is normal for a challenger. He struggles to achieve self-control and self-containment but emotions start building beyond what is appropriate, and the challenger has trouble pulling himself together.

Escalators go from point A to point Z without seeing any possibilities in between. This is exemplified by the mother of 12-year-old Jake. Margo was supposed to call his school and clear a tardy, but she forgot. When Jake found out, he was sure his grades would suffer, affect his college entrance, and perhaps his entire life. He saw his whole world falling apart over one tardy!

What fuels the escalation is the feeling that things are getting out of control. If Jake can anticipate problems before they happen, then they can be prevented, but each anticipated problem causes the escalation to increase. It becomes a vicious circle.

An escalator goes into a **defensive modality.** The child sticks to one detail in the conversation and tunes out everything else you are saying. For example, Jake kept repeating, "You promised to call. You promised to call." When a child is feeling vulnerable, overtired, cranky, or cornered, his sense of identity is threatened, and he escalates as a way of protecting himself. The child becomes so defensive and overwhelmed that whatever you say is useless.

That's why it is important to get to your child's inner world when he starts to escalate.

In order to "reach" your escalator, here are some ways to diffuse the situation.

Parent Plan

- Identify for yourself the conflict of agendas between parent and child. Have you made too many demands one after the other? Are you in a bad mood? Has your child been pushed too far?
- Hold your child if she's in a tantrum mode, but don't talk.
- When your child is calm, offer to help her work out the problem.
- Don't light a match to an explosive. Escalators, because they often have self-control problems, don't do well when pushed beyond their emotional capabilities. If your child is overtired, hyper, or in an escalation mode, wait until she is ready to receive what you have to say.
- Be direct. Be consistent with your request. Do not ask more than twice. Do not yell.
- Retreat calmly. Walk away before the child has escalated to hysteria.

NEGOTIATORS

A clever negotiator can leave a parent drained and exhausted. Parents will often get worn down by the child's nagging and eventually give in just to appease him and stop the demands. This only reinforces the challenging negotiator. Appeasement can act as a reward for inappropriate behavior.

Parents may resent their own inability to say "no" and become very angry when they feel manipulated. There is a fine line between being inflexible and being fair, but an agreement based on some consistent guidelines must be reached between parent and child.

Ten-year-old Amy begged her mother for cookies at 3:30 p.m. on the way home from school. Amy clearly knew that the rule was no sugary foods, and certainly not before dinner. Amy's mother, Leslie, said, "No," but Amy negotiated. She begged. She pleaded. She cajoled. Then Amy, the yapper, used clever psychology.

"But mom, I'm not fat. I don't have cavities, and I don't eat a lot of sweets. Other kids' parents let them!"

Leslie finally gave in. She stopped at the market and bought Amy chocolate cookies. That night Leslie was furious with her daughter. She took away T.V. privileges for three days, and Amy was totally perplexed. She didn't understand the punishment, let alone the crime.

Once they get their way, challenging negotiators appear satisfied. They go on about their business until the next situation arises.

Parental Challenge with Negotiators

Leslie needs to look at why saying "no" is so hard for her. In the interaction with Amy, saying "yes" only led to her resentment later. Leslie could have simply but firmly said, "I'm not willing to talk about it."

If the parent, like Leslie, does give in and feels angry later, it is important to express these feelings directly. Leslie could have gone to Amy's room later that night and said, "I made a mistake. I didn't help you today. I was trying to help you set limits and boundaries about what you eat, and I stopped at a store and bought you sugary cookies, which aren't good for you. I wanted to please you. I'm going to make every effort not to break this rule again. I love you and want what's best for you."

These responses don't just teach a behavior, they also help a child understand what motivates behavior. You are telling your child that you sometimes make mistakes, but you can also correct them.

Parent Plan

- If you feel boxed in by your child, immediately stop the negotiations by saying, "I will think it over and let you know later." If your child does not accept your response, walk away.
- Avoid a win-lose situation so anger and resentment don't build up.
- It is important to support your child's thought process without losing control. For instance, you might say to your negotiator, "I'll consider what you have to say, but I may not change my mind," or "I respect what you have to say, but you need to accept my decision."

CURIOSITY SEEKERS

Curious challengers are acutely aware of their five senses. They want to taste, touch, hear, see, and smell everything. Curiosity seekers are not aware of boundaries. They may have trouble sitting still and listening attentively.

One worried mother of a toddler was sure there was

something terribly wrong with her three-year-old girl. During "Mommy and Me" class, all of the other children were listening to the teacher sing songs, but Candice was rummaging through the teacher's bag, looking at the other instruments, checking out the paintings on the wall, and touching all the books. The teacher wasn't too happy. Ann kept yelling at Candice, warning her that she had to listen, but the girl acted totally uninterested. That night, Candice was singing all the songs that the teacher taught that day.

Ann was incredulous. How could Candice know these songs? She wasn't even listening. But, in truth, the child was listening—*her way*. Children are not clones. Every youngster has a different way of receiving information. In this case, Candice needed to be engaged in an active way. She was not a passive learner, but a kinesthetic learner. (Learning styles will be discussed in Chapter 2.) She did not need to focus on the teacher to hear or learn from her.

Parent Plan

- Curiosity seekers often need to learn by natural consequences. Telling them a thousand times not to do something is often useless. Unfortunately, curious challengers can sometimes face difficult consequences for their actions in order to learn. Hopefully, these consequences are neither harmful nor dangerous.

  For example, one nine-year-old boasted that she could find her mitten in the snow every time she buried it. She kept challenging herself by pushing her curiosity. Finally, she had the great idea of hiding her glove deep in the snow, and spinning herself around until she fell over from dizziness. You can imagine the natural consequences—no more glove and a lot of hysteria. But telling her not to bury the glove would have been useless.

- Be supportive. Channel your child's curiosity in positive ways. Say, "I think it's great that you are so interested in everything. Let's go outside and explore the park."
- Set safe limits and be firm when safety rules are broken.

COMPETITIVE

Being #1 is everything to a competitive challenger. She is like the pusher in that regard. If you observe an elementary school class for a day, watch which kids push in the front of the line, call out the answers in class, run for a front row seat, and get into the cafeteria first. Chances are, the competitive challenger is leading the way.

Healthy competition is great. It can motivate and stimulate children. But challengers are so focused on the outcome of the competition that they don't enjoy themselves. Thus, these children can set themselves up for failure, because they can't always win.

A competitor's need to win creates so much anxiety over his performance that it can inhibit his ability to learn. The key to helping a competitor succeed is to stimulate intrinsic motivation. We'll talk more about that in Chapter 2.

Competitive challengers can be winners—with your help.

Parent Plan

- Stress intrinsic motivation. Don't set up a competition. If there is competition, it should be with the child himself to do the best he can.
- Value the way your child looks at something. Teach love of learning. For instance, stress the pleasure of a good story not just how well it is read. Is your child animated? Can he describe the characters? Can he tell you what it's about?
- Help your child focus on the effort, not the outcome. Reward effort. In Chapter 6 we will discuss the value of noncompetitive play.
- Look at your own style of learning and how you communicate it to your child. (We will discuss this in Chapter 2.)
- Never compare your child with others. We all learn differently. We all have different abilities.
- If your child constantly has difficulty with motivation, it may indicate some underlying learning disability that needs to be addressed.
- Build up your child's self-esteem by supporting her efforts.

EASILY FRUSTRATED

Many of us have grown up in a world of immediate gratification. We have also raised our children that way.

When success is not immediate, the challenger becomes self-critical.

It is painful for this kind of child when he doesn't win or get his way. What is missing is an understanding of the building blocks to success. A key component of those building blocks is to reward the small steps taken toward achieving a goal. And each small achievement is rewarding in and of itself.

It's necessary to teach the frustrated challenger how to accept delayed gratification and stand up to the pressures for immediate gratification that our culture perpetuates. This is no small task, since a child is bombarded with the promise of a quick solution to his every conflict.

Your child's feelings about himself are at stake when he is frustrated. If he can't solve a problem quickly, he'll give up or start to escalate. Unfortunately, in the world inside and outside the family, immediate gratification is rarely attainable, so frustration builds up, especially for an impatient challenger.

Communication has a domino effect. A parental "no" can lead to a parent/challenger nightmare that links many of the traits together.

"No"

|

negotiation

|

manipulation

|

pushing

|

escalation

|

World War III

The key is to work with the frustrated challenger early. The child may have trouble tolerating what he views as his weak spots and become anxious. This may affect his ability to learn from his mistakes and tolerate frustration. He may want to excel in everything, but has difficulty facing his limits. A challenger has trouble tolerating being just average or mediocre. So frustration builds up when the child falls back and then judges himself as a failure.

Parent Plan

- Work step-by-step with your child and reward each small success as you go. This will teach delayed gratification. If your child is being patient when you are busy, tell him, "You are so patient. I'm proud of you. Now, I am happy to help you."
- Let your child know you can't be good at everything.
- Don't be judgmental. Children feel parental criticism and judge themselves harshly. If your child is having trouble mastering a task, be encouraging, don't tell him how easy it is or criticize him.

- Stress perseverance. When one dad waited in line for two hours to get tickets to a much desired basketball game, he displayed patience and perseverance. Use good role modeling.
- Teach children about delayed gratification by using yourself and the world as role models. For example, your child should know that you go to work, you get paid at the end of the month, and you can't buy things until you get paid.
- Teach your challenger how to problem solve. (We will discuss this in chapter 3.)

STRONG-WILLED

"Strong-willed" is a term often tossed around regarding children. We tend to think that strong-willed children are purposefully being stubborn or mean, but it's just not that simple. No child sets out to be oppositional. For a strong-willed child, anything can become a power struggle. Opinions, likes, and dislikes are all a potential source of conflict.

Sometimes the strong will emanates from fear—fear of change, fear of failure, and a fear of things happening out of one's control. A challenger needs to maintain his sense of identity by being oppositional and resistant. Challengers get fixated on certain possessions or behaviors because they need to feel safe and in control.

One little boy would only eat pizza at Shakey's when he went out with his parents. If they went anywhere else, he wouldn't eat. He needed to control his world. Change is so threatening for the strong-willed challenger that he fights to stay in the safe zone.

The fear a challenger faces often immobilizes him to change even the simplest things. For the challenger, change is not just different, it's worse. The thought that something different may be okay is a large leap. The thought that change may actually be wonderful is often unfathomable! It's as if the word "change" means "bad." The task here is for the child to learn—in small steps—that change can have a positive outcome.

Susie is a child whose strong will had a negative impact. In her second grade class, each table worked in teams of four. Yet, Susie never wanted to go along with her table's choices. She preferred working independently. She didn't want to share her materials, and resisted the team's goals. Her teacher was upset and tried to get her to comply. The team members were furious with her. The overall team's performance on group projects suffered because of Susie's strong-willed attitude.

Parent Plan

- Understanding your child's world and why he reacts the way he does is the key to establishing a better relationship. The strong-willed child is not just being oppositional, but rather is attempting to get his needs met.
- Try to diminish the power struggle by giving your child choices. For instance, when your strong-willed child asks for cookies, ask her, "How many are enough?" Try to see how your child organizes her world. Respect her

reasonable choices. If it seems unreasonable, be honest and say, "I'm not comfortable with you eating twelve cookies. It's not healthy. Come up with another plan." This experience will help you see what kind of boundaries your child sets for herself. It also teaches her responsibility.

ENERGETIC

Do you have the feeling your child is like a Duracell battery? He keeps going and going and going while all the others have wound down. When everyone else seems to be getting tired, your energetic challenger says, "Okay, what are we doing next?"

Challengers have trouble closing down their motor or shifting gears. Their energy level gets so great that they have no sense of inner limits. They become frustrated by the inability to relax and grow even more upset. Their sense of self-control is weakened. This brings with it a feeling of reduced self-esteem.

Parent Plan

- Plan activities carefully. Limit the length of each activity.
- Build in rewards that will help your child shift gears. For example, say, "At sleep time, I'll read you a special book."
- Give your child advance notice of what will take place. "We will leave when the timer goes off." Challengers

need a marker. If you don't use a timer, put on a record. When the record is over say, "It's time to go to bed."

- Help your child change gears the first few times to guide him into the finished task. For instance, if he is working on a school project and you see he is having trouble completing it, offer to help him—look up words, organize his papers, or read it for mistakes.
- Routines are essential. Plan your child's schedule and try to consistently stick to it. It's the ritual that creates a calming effect on children.
- Ask your child for suggestions on how she could wind down. Don't expect a long list—one or two will suffice.
- If you set up a chart of chores, focus on just a few tasks at a time. Let your child see the value in the completed tasks so that she can gain success before moving on to a new activity.

Energizers need help focusing. Work together as a team. Don't just say, "Clean your room," and expect to see it happen. Show your child how to make the bed, or do it together. Make a game out of picking up toys. Reward the clean room with a lot of praise.

IMPATIENT AND NOT EASILY SATISFIED

How many times do you recall your challenger saying, "What's next? I want more. Can I have another one?"

Why can't this child get filled up? Why can't he be grateful for what he does have and not resentful for what he doesn't?

Challengers are often impatient and seemingly insatiable. They want immediate gratification, and they are afraid they are missing out on something if they don't get it.

The insatiable feeling comes out of the belief that if they *get* more they will *be* more. A challenger's self-esteem often rides the wave of wanting more only to be disappointed by hitting the shore of life's limits.

It is important to help your child so he will ultimately feel more satisfied with making choices and knowing that there are limits. Unconsciously, parents and society perpetuate the importance of "things" to children. Television and the media communicate the "more-more" theory. Commercials entice children. "If you get another toy, another special food, you'll be happy." Children who are easily frustrated internalize these pressures.

For example, no matter what Kim's mom bought her, she seemed dissatisfied. If Paula bought a toy Kim wanted, she would point out one she liked better. Or she would set the toy down, as if it had no significance, and ask her mother, "What else will you buy me?"

This happened when Paula bought her clothing, as well as when she took Kim out for a special evening. If Paula bought Kim one dress, she wanted another. If they went to MacDonald's, Kim wanted to know why they didn't go to Jack-in-the-Box. Clearly, Paula felt frustrated and was getting angry. She called Kim a spoiled brat. But in truth, Kim was just being herself. Her challenging nature expressed itself in an inability to be satisfied.

Another mother decided to take her six-year-old to see a movie. Lisa had the entire day planned—a movie and lunch. While standing in line, Abbie became whiny and demanding.

She said she didn't want to stand in line. She just wanted to go to the Disney store and see the movie later.

Lisa became angry and disappointed. Here she had planned on such a nice day, and her daughter had ruined it.

At this point, Lisa should have offered Abbie a choice—either to wait in line and see the movie *or* go to the Disney Store, and save the movie for another day. It then would become Abbie's choice, and Lisa need not feel emotionally hooked in and frustrated.

Similarly, Paula should have offered Kim a choice. That way the child takes responsibility. A parent of a challenger needs to recognize that her needs may be different from her child's.

Parent Plan

- Avoid unrealistic expectations. It's okay for your child to ask for things.
- Identify for yourself what you are prepared to give your child.
- Give your child choices. It's not what you do, it's the quality of the interaction that reduces the insatiable feeling. Choices help your child feel more in control.
- You cannot punish your child for your expectations or disappointments. Not every child will like what you like or act how you *think* he should act. It's better to say to your child, "I'm sorry you don't want to see the movie. I thought you would enjoy it. Maybe another time."
- Set limits for what is appropriate and comfortable for you. For example, if you can't afford to buy your child

Nintendo, then be honest. Plan together to save for the desired toy and set a goal.

- Ask your child, "What would fill you up? Ten toys? Twenty toys? One hundred toys?" Parents can say, "It would be wonderful to get everything you want." Acknowledge the feeling and let your child know that the *feeling*, the desire, is okay.

The ultimate goal of the parent plan is to help you learn to teach your challenger how to set boundaries and limits, make choices, and acknowledge others' feelings. By giving your challenging child positive methods that focus on his particular needs, you will be assisting him in feeling good about himself—the ultimate gift for a challenging child.

2

Parents—The Challenged

As a parent of a challenging child you often wonder if you are a good parent. You may be plagued with guilt—what did I do wrong? Why does my child act this way? **WHY ME?**

You blame yourself for your child's troubles in school, then resent the child for the guilt you feel. Anger and frustration seem to accompany challenged parents—especially if they are ill prepared and uninformed about their challenger—because these are tough kids to raise. They require more of everything—more attention, discipline, energy, understanding, and time.

BLAME

The first challenge you may face is to move away from blaming your child, the school, society, or yourself. Move toward problem solving. This is a profound struggle because, the world around you may judge you by your child's behavior.

Blame solves nothing and ultimately antagonizes and jeopardizes intimate relationships with your child.

Although you are not to blame for your child's challenging behavior, you do play a role in managing and ultimately creating a happier and stronger relationship with him. You have to analyze your own, as well as your child's, motivations and behavior in order to understand why you may be having so much trouble with your challenger.

You may have distinctly different needs from your child. A challenger often refuses to go along with your needs or desires. He challenges the parental role on every issue, and constant battles ensue. Then you and your spouse may blame each other for being unsupportive, inconsistent, or unwilling to set limits.

As a challenged parent, out of anxiety, you may raise your children with a lot of "shoulds." You may look to the outside world, other parents and children, your own parents, books, T.V.—anything— to help with the anxiety.

If your child does not compare to these outside standards you may fear that you will be judged by his actions. You may unconsciously feel that your child is a reflection of yourself. Our children's behavior stirs up many surprising feelings and we may overreact. But instead of placing blame, look for solutions. This chapter will guide you in finding some.

CONFLICT IN PARENT/CHILD LEARNING STYLES

So how do parents determine if they are overreacting to their children's behavior?

In Chapter 1, you identified your challenging child's

traits. Now it is useful to learn about the seven different types of intelligence. By doing so, you will be able to further understand your own behavior and how it affects your challenger. If you discover that your child has a different learning style than your own, rather than butting heads all the time, you will be better equipped to alter your interactions in order to adapt to his needs.

Of course, no individual is composed of just one type of intelligence. Most of us are a composite of many different types. But the general way we approach learning and people is often focused in one way. Let's look at the seven types of intelligence and the aptitudes they create, based on the book *Frames of Mind* by noted Harvard psychologist Howard Gardner.

SEVEN TYPES OF INTELLIGENCE

- **Linguistic Intelligence** These individuals use or play with words. They learn foreign languages easily, are good at riddles and rhymes, and like to read.
- **Logical Intelligence** They pursue complex sequences of ideas, enjoy math and puzzles,—especially solving problems in their heads. They like chess, mind benders, and are organized.
- **Spatial Intelligence** These people have acute visual memory, and are artistic. They perceive the world accurately and reproduce or alter that perception. They like to invent, build, do mazes, or jigsaw puzzles.
- **Bodily-Kinetic Intelligence** They are athletic, and aware of their body in space. They move with skill and grace.

They respond to test questions with gut feelings rather than logic.

- **Musical Intelligence** They recognize rhythm, pitch, meter, and tone. They can determine when sounds are off-key, and remember information by having heard it rather than reading it.
- **Interpersonal Intelligence** They have great social skills, understand emotions of others, and communicate well. They are good speakers, and form many friendships. Being good leaders, they mediate arguments among friends.
- **Intrapersonal Intelligence** They have great understanding of their emotions. They are less gregarious, and are more apt to pursue individual activities. They are introspective, focusing on dreams and emotions. They can learn and work independently.

Mozart, for instance, was singularly musical. A great athlete like Michael Jordan possesses bodily-kinetic intelligence. Whereas a psychologist might have a deep understanding of himself and, therefore, possess intrapersonal intelligence, a politician would more likely possess interpersonal intelligence, reflected in her ability to interact with lots of people in an easygoing and comfortable manner. See if you can recognize the learning styles of yourself and your child.

WHAT IS YOURS AND YOUR CHILD'S LEARNING STYLES?

Parents' Intelligence		_Child's Intelligence_
Musical	☐	☐
Bodily-Kinetic	☐	☐
Logical	☐	☐
Intrapersonal	☐	☐
Interpersonal	☐	☐
Spatial	☐	☐
Linguistic	☐	☐

* Check the boxes that apply

An example of two conflicting types of intelligence and how they affect a challenger and her parent is the story of eight-year-old Jenny. Jenny's mother Doris was upset because Jenny would watch T.V., dance, sing, and dawdle every morning before school. Doris was a **logical learner** and expected Jenny to put on her clothes and her shoes, brush her hair and her teeth, and eat her breakfast efficiently without dawdling or having to be told to hurry up.

Jenny on the other hand, did everything backwards. She wanted to watch television in the morning. She insisted that watching T.V. helped her get dressed. She'd dance, and put on her clothes slowly, singing happily. She never got dressed the same way twice and she and her mom fought endlessly. While Doris demanded control, Jenny did things her own way.

Because Doris was a logical learner, she pursued life in a logical sequence. She was highly organized. Routines made sense to her.

Jenny on the other hand, was a free spirit. Her way of approaching situations was more **bodily-kinetic.** She responded to the world with her gut feeling rather than logic or a desire for routine.

Doris was challenged to look at her own life and experiences. She realized that she fell back into a parenting style like her own mother—rigid and demanding. When she became aware that Jenny's approach to doing things was different— not a sign of being obstinate—she was able to loosen up and make a compromise that was agreeable to both of them.

The slow process of helping your challenger begins with helping yourself contain and understand your own feelings.

For instance, Lara, twelve, was seen as challenging by her parents, because she was only interested in playing the violin. Her father wanted her to develop other intellectual skills, and perhaps, become a lawyer, like himself. To Ted, playing the violin, was only worthwhile as a hobby.

Because of her **musical intelligence,** Lara was highly sensitive to sound, tone, and pitch. She preferred to learn new things by memorizing how they sounded. When Ted would explain things, it seemed to Lara as if he were yelling or raising his voice. Lara could not get through to her father and became upset and anxious around him. Eventually, she developed a physical reaction to Ted's voice—she "closed down" and stopped listening, which made things worse.

As you see, Lara's learning style was musical. The more she withdrew, the more Ted seemed to yell and place demands on her. In contrast, Ted's style was **logical** and **linguistic**. He was familiar with dealing with people in a courtroom setting where both his commanding voice and his ability to explain an issue in a logical manner were highly valued.

Lara and Ted just kept missing each other because of their different intellectual styles and different forms of expression. They each had trouble entering the other's world. Eventually, through counseling, Ted learned to understand Lara's sensitivities and differing styles. For example, Ted learned to write down things he wanted to discuss with her so that she could read them beforehand, thereby avoiding the "yelling" problem. By understanding each other's unique styles, they learned to work together, support each other, and share in each other's world.

As in Lara's situation, conflicts between parents and children often arise simply because each sees the world so differently. Parents can deprive their children of their natural talents and intelligences because of what they think their children should be doing. By understanding each other's unique learning styles and intelligences, parents can guide, develop, and support their children's talents and goals.

EXTROVERTS VS. INTROVERTS

Introverts are introspective and enjoy being alone. They are comfortable doing solitary tasks. Conversely, extroverts thrive in the outer world of people and get nourished by social relationships. They relax by being with people and are often gregarious.

An introverted parent would most likely view her extroverted child as "hyper," while an extroverted parent might be critical of an introverted child who may appear to be shy and withdrawn. The extroverted parent may ask her child, "Why can't you be more social?"

Of course, there is not a "better" way to be. These are just different personality traits. An introverted parent may view his high-spirited, active child as challenging simply because his way of approaching the world is in opposition to his child's.

We tend to judge people who are different from ourselves and often attempt to change them to be more like ourselves simply because "our way" feels more comfortable. But trying to change your child's innate character is neither possible nor desirable. A child may forego his true solitary or introverted interests, like story writing, in order to gain parental approval by being social and extroverted.

One family's conflict demonstrates how a parent who pressures his introverted child to partake in an extroverted activity can completely turn that child off to that activity.

Hal was the quintessential sports lover. He watched sports, played sports, and expected his son, nine-year-old Jake, to do the same. But Jake did not like sports, and had no real interest in pursuing them. Jake preferred to partake in quiet solitary things like reading and computers.

Hal was upset. He tried to force Jake into playing Little League, which only undermined their relationship.

The more Hal demanded, the more Jake fought against him. Hal thought Jake was stubborn and defiant. He could not understand their differences.

The relationship deteriorated. Hal, in consultation with me, finally acknowledged that Jake would never win trophies for baseball, but would receive recognition for his science projects.

Hal, by understanding his son's unique personality traits, was able to rebuild his relationship with Jake.

RESPECTING NEEDS AND DIFFERENCES

Children are not duplicates of their parents, especially challenging children. When your toddler first broke away from you, it wasn't just the terrible two's, it was his way of saying, "I'm separate from you. I'm my own person."

This concept is difficult for many parents, because it means they have to give up some control, and let their child make mistakes and even sometimes fail. This is not an easy task, especially if a parent sees his child's failure as his own. Often parents have a desire to rescue their children from mistakes they have made.

Parents can unconsciously contribute to their challenger's problems through their own behavior. Critical parental attitudes negatively impact on children's creativity and spontaneity. Dr. Teresa Amabile has constructed a list to help you realistically assess your behaviors toward your child. Respect your child's differences. It *is* difficult to let go, but in the end you derive great satisfaction from your independent, self-motivated, creative, and happier child.

PARENTAL BEHAVIORS LIST

Overcontrol A parent who tells his child exactly how to do things all the time is overcontrolling and can inhibit originality and exploration.

Surveillance This is when a parent overmonitors a child's activities. For example, if a child is coloring and draws a tree out of proportion, the parent may want to jump in and correct his drawing. This attitude inhibits a child's risk-taking creative urges.

Restricting choices A parent may want to teach the correct way to do something instead of letting his child use his own imagination and sense of curiosity. One mom restricted her daughter's Barbie play to the doll house, but the little girl wanted to use the entire bedroom and bathroom. It would have been better to let her child use her imagination unrestrictedly.

Pressure Every parent thinks his child is a star athlete and an A student. But this is not the case. It's important to be sensitive to the developmental ability of your child and build his sense of self-esteem.

Competition Parents often set up unrealistic expectations for their children. For example, unless the child wins an art contest, his drawing is dismissed. This creates a feeling of right or wrong, win or lose. The child is set up to be overly concerned about winning rather than enjoying the activity.

Evaluation This refers to making comparisons. Parents might compare their child's work to one of his friend's. They may be overly concerned about what the teacher or relatives will say, rather than indicating that his work is "fine" as it is, and letting him enjoy it.

Rewards The love of learning and enjoying the effort should be the end reward, not material gifts or money. It's important to give positive feedback and reinforcement, rather than a dollar, for every A.

RELATIONSHIP CHALLENGE

United Front

"One for all, and all for one . . ." has a lot more meaning for challenged parents than for the Three Musketeers. It should be a parental priority to create a united front when raising a challenging child.

A challenger can pull parents in different directions by his demanding behavior. One parent prefers flexibility in order to defuse conflicts and avoid escalation. The other parent believes setting clear limits with consequences reduces the chance of escalation. Both are right in different situations. The mixed message rather than the choice of intervention may actually create the problem. Worst of all, parents may blame each other. Presenting a united front on a case by case basis teaches cooperation and compromise.

One father refused to acknowledge that there was any problem with his challenging child. He kept insisting that his son was fine. He said, "He'll grow out of it." The mother insisted something was not right with the family dynamics. How do you deal with these differing points of view?

Parents give children mixed messages by not creating a united front. One parent's attempt to control the child's behavior can increase conflict in the family. For example, if John is too noisy and it bothers your wife but not you, do you ask John to quiet down and risk further explosions or say nothing and irritate your wife? You are in essence choosing to avoid conflict. This situation again gives mixed messages to your child. The next time you're out with him you might allow him to be noisy. He is not really sure what's expected of him. When the child alternately sides with one parent or the other, it creates anxiety, tension, confusion, and conflict.

Parents need to decide together and ahead of time just how *they* are going to discipline *their* child. Your relationship with your spouse is one of the most important elements of child rearing. You need to talk about your backgrounds and beliefs regarding discipline and problem solving. Does the relationship value working together or just giving it lip service? Are you willing to compromise? What happens to your ability to compromise when the various problems of child rearing arise?

Parents' preconceived notions of what's appropriate for the child may be a source of conflict. Mothers and fathers need to be able to work out an arrangement that makes the child's issues—and how they are dealt with—clear and acceptable to everyone.

Issues often arise that are not about the child but about our own childhood conflicts. For instance, when a mother and father were fighting over whether to take a blanket away from their three-year-old boy, the father, not understanding the importance of transitional objects, thought of the blanket as he was taught to in his own childhood—that little boys don't have blankets because they need to be independent and strong.

A child can become a pawn in the clash between two different parenting styles, and the conflict that arises can ultimately affect the parents' closeness. The source of this clash is often the dual need to feel in control of the child and one's spouse's reaction to his difficult behavior. The end result is that everyone feels rejected, and the child is pulled between both parents.

The goal of a united front is to compromise and to break

negative parental behavior patterns. Compromise is sometimes viewed as lose-lose rather than win-win, but the true value of compromise is that it increases intimacy. By listening to and acknowledging your mate's ideas and feelings, you will come closer to creating a more effective parental bond.

POWER STRUGGLES AND CONTROL ISSUES

Nothing is more familiar to a challenged parent than power struggles. Challengers push and pull, put up defenses, and fight to get their own way. For a strong-willed or controlling parent, this can lead to big problems. Your household will turn into a battlefield—fights, yelling, frustration, and an unhappy parent-child relationship—if you don't handle power struggles effectively.

Someone has to be willing to "give in," to "let go." But when you are so focused on rules being followed to the letter, you are destined to encounter resistance. Challengers want their own way. But by constantly butting heads with your child, you only create more resistance. It's the simple analogy, "If there is no wall to run into, then the car won't crash." This is not to say you should allow your child to do what he wants. There have to be clear limits and boundaries established and a consistent enforcement of these boundaries.

Control can revolve around any issue that becomes important for parents. You have to decide what is worth fighting over. You can create conflict over anything. The family needs to establish what's most important: hygiene, safety, socialization, learning. Parents need to prioritize.

Respect what's developmentally appropriate for your

child. For instance, you wouldn't expect a three-year-old to make his bed, but you would expect it of an eight-year-old.

A child is not necessarily challenging because he goes through certain developmental stages. A parent can mistake this normal behavior for opposition or defiance. For example, sometimes you might think that the "terrible two's," when a child constantly says "no," is a challenge to parental authority. In actuality, this is a normal stage of development. The child is experiencing the need to separate, a need to seek out her own identity.

At four to six years of age, children go through an emotional transformation. Girls may become clingy and very attached to their fathers. Boys often become competitive with their fathers and possessive of their mothers. A parent—feeling rejected—might react with criticism or disapproval. Once again, this is developmentally appropriate behavior: the Oedipal stage. Children outgrow it as long as the parent is understanding, loving, and does not take any of the child's actions personally.

School-age children are trying to master skills like reading and writing, as well as developing new thinking skills. You may be judgmental and critical as your child struggles to learn new tasks that you find simple. If he doesn't do well on a test, you might want to correct him immediately. But this is a developmental stage where your child needs support, because he is trying to learn to think logically, in a literal, organized manner.

When you let go of needing to control everything, it improves the parent/child relationship and diminishes power struggles. Ask yourself: Isn't your relationship with your child more important than having all the ducks lined up in a row?

Is not taking a bath every day going to cause your child to never bathe as an adult?

There has to be cooperative problem solving rather than doing everything by the book. By letting a child make decisions about innocuous issues like where he stores his Power Rangers helps teach responsibility, and transfers some of the control off the parent.

If a parent hovers over his son rather than letting him do his own homework and work out the problems himself, the boy is not learning from his own efforts. But if the child does his own work and he gets some wrong answers, then he'll learn to correct himself.

Learn to let go! We repeat this concept many times throughout the book because it is such a valuable lesson.

POSITIVE VS. NEGATIVE ATTENTION

Challengers, by their very nature, can try the nerves of even the most patient parent. It's one thing to have us suggest that you be patient and positive toward your child but it's quite another matter when, on a day-to-day basis, you're pulling your hair out. But challenging kids, often bright and intuitive, will find a way to get what they want. Often that's attention, and they will use negative behavior, like pulling the dogs tail, if it works. Challengers become accustomed to "negative attention," and it creates a comfort zone for them. This is best demonstrated by Andy whose misbehaving will cause his mother to yell, scream, and stop what she's doing to spend a good part of an hour talking, pleading, and putting all the focus on him.

Of course, children don't consciously think about these things, but unconsciously they are achieving what they want—getting attention in familiar ways. Parents need to turn this negative mind-set around. Your aim should be for your child to learn to thrive on positive attention.

Parent Plan

First of all, you need to be aware that you are giving negative attention. As soon as your child does something that warrants your attention:

- Stop and look at your child, but say nothing. Take a deep breath.
- Ask your child, "Is there something you need?" or "Please wait, and I'll be glad to help you when I get off the phone."
- Leave the room if you find your patience wearing thin.

Focus on:
- What the child does well and **reward good behavior often.**
- Ignore some negative behaviors that are not destructive.
- Use time-outs or removal of privileges rather than hitting or yelling.
- Include your child in some decisions and choices. Make sure he feels like part of the family—not just a troublemaker.

OPPOSITIONAL INDEPENDENCE

A challenger's identity is wrapped up in his saying "no" to your "yes" or getting you to say "yes" when you really want to say "no." Oppositionality may come up around activities that you want for him like camping. Your child may feel pushed by you, while you are simply trying to set up the rules or make a new plan or offer him an enjoyable experience. In fact, he may even want the chance to go camping but because you want it, he decides he doesn't. This same attitude can, unfortunately, carry over into their responses regarding rules and limits.

Challengers often view limits as a rejection rather than a source of comfort, as most children would. Rules may create a great deal of anxiety. Challengers are afraid they won't measure up to what's expected of them. This spills over into school.

Many children know intuitively what is expected of them and follow the rules. But a challenger has trouble identifying his inner process. He may experience the world differently. He has trouble expressing his emotional states in words, so he gets frustrated easily and his typical response is to escalate.

It's necessary to form a team with your child so he doesn't think that you are personally imposing rules to punish him. Depersonalize limits. Let him know that everyone has rules to follow and they are not a form of rejection or disapproval. For example, we all stop at red lights to prevent accidents. Family discussions are vital to learning what's bothering the child. Everyone needs to take part and be open about problems in the family dynamics. This will help pinpoint the mechanisms that trigger the child's oppositional behavior.

Parent Plan

Ask the following questions of your child in an attempt to discover your child's inner world. This is the start to reducing opposition.

- Do we bug you about too many things?
- What bothers you when we propose a new situation? What are you afraid of?
- What did I say that upset you? Was it the way I said it?
- How can we talk about this so we can come to a solution?
- Let's play hot potato/cold potato. As I get close to what you were feeling, say, "hot" or "cold."
- I'm guessing you thought you'd disappoint me if you wouldn't measure up. Is this true?"

Parents need to find out what way is the best way to help their child respond to the above questions. Try using dolls or stuffed animals. For example, act out with the dolls what happens when you get upset. You can also try drawings. For example say, "Draw what your worst fear is if you had to go to camp without a friend."

You may not have a major breakthrough, but just playing with your child will give you both a source of comfort, and he'll feel validated because you are showing you care about his feelings. Let him know that you want to respond to him in a more thoughtful way.

- Try to catch yourself once you have made inappropriate remarks or started a needless power struggle. The important thing is to recognize where *you* are coming from.

- Sit down with your child and share personal stories about your own life. Say, "I want you to know more about me."
- Although this dialogue may be difficult at first, inevitably it will open the lines of communication and build a stronger relationship.

With a challenger, you might think that you are not being "heard" when you have this conversation, but don't let that deter you. Your concern and care are being heard in your challenger's own way. You are planting seeds for the future and building the mutual respect that will last you and your child a lifetime.

DIFFERING AGENDAS

There are a lot of mixed messages around agendas. Each parent has a different agenda for his child because of conditioning from his own childhood. You experience your child in one way and probably have certain expectations about how you hope she'll act. But your child may not act according to how you wish she will behave. The "wished for experience" becomes a conflict between parent and child. This can be true around issues of manners.

Let's look at Madison and her mom's differing agendas. Jan asked Madison to eat breakfast before she left the house for school. So seven-year-old Madison took her fingers and dove into a plate of leftover spaghetti in the refrigerater and said, "Okay, I ate breakfast."

Jan was furious, yelling to Madison that her manners were horrible and that spaghetti wasn't a healthy breakfast. Madison was confused. She thought eating something—anything at all—would please her mom, and she didn't even consider how she went about eating it.

Tom told Jan not to make an issue of it and dismissed the whole thing. Later that night, when Madison went to pour catsup on her plate and a giant glob came out, Tom became furious because she was wasting catsup. Madison thought she was pouring the catsup so well. She couldn't win with either of her parents.

When challengers feels cornered by no-win situations, they start to escalate into hysterical behavior. Clearly Madison's agenda was different from her parents. She just wanted to eat. Jan and Tom believed she should do so with a certain decorum. Madison became frustrated, angry, and insecure. This set the stage for her to escalate.

Let's look at how these agendas could be altered. You need to consider the negative aspects of pressing your personal agendas on your child by asking yourself the following questions:

- Is my child acting age-appropriate?
- Is my goal realistic?
- Am I conveying a mixed message?
- What is the real motivation behind my request? Does it have to do with my own feelings of discomfort and need for control?

- What impact does my reaction have on my child's self-esteem?

You can look at Madison's actions in two ways. For instance, eating the spaghetti is an attempt to comply with her mother's request, and putting the catsup on the plate was an attempt to master a skill.

But Jan and Tom assumed that Madison was wasting catsup, which wastes money, and that eating the spaghetti with her fingers was a purposeful act of bad manners. Neither of these acts had a negative meaning to Madison.

This example underscores the many ways in which parents may impose their agenda on their child, although the child's agenda is quite different, and not meant to create a negative impact. Give yourself and your child a break. Be realistic about your requests. Use positive reinforcement. Tell your child how much you appreciate her attempt at pouring the catsup and her desire to eat breakfast all by herself.

FLEXIBILITY

There is constantly a choice a parent has to make with a challenger: Do I tolerate my child's anxieties, or do I accede to his request because at the moment, it's not worth a fight?

Lynn was at the library with her seven-year-old Samantha, when her daughter asked how to spell a word. Lynn said, "You try to spell it. You know how to." Samantha got very upset. She raised her voice. "I can't do it. I can't do it. Just spell it for me, Mom!"

Lynn decided to spell the word, rather than engage in

a power struggle. Demanding Samantha spell the word would only have created enormous tension over a simple problem.

The hard work for you is to know when to acquiesce to a request, in order to reduce your child's sense of frustration, embarrassment, and loss of control. The difficulty lies in containing and controlling your own anxieties. You need to weigh each situation carefully and pick your fights.

Some challengers have anticipatory anxiety about failing, the unknown, and new situations. Be gentle, go slowly, don't push or demand.

Tommy's dad Bill was very late getting to work and getting him to school. Grace was yelling at Bill. Bill was yelling at Tommy, who was nervous and crying. Nevertheless, Tommy kept dawdling, which only made Bill angrier. A major family argument ensued.

It's important to contain yourself in the same way that you are teaching your challenger to contain himself. In this situation, it's important to call a time-out. (See Chapter 3.)

Parent Plan

- Stop and look at emotional choices and acknowledge your feelings. Bill could say, "I'm late and upset and I'm sorry I'm taking it out on you."
- Ask yourself, how should I handle this situation? "Let's all take a time-out and I'll call my office and tell them I'll be late."

- Try to find a way to salvage some good feelings toward your child by focusing on what you've all learned.

Doing the unexpected with your challenging child can sometimes surprise and delight. One dad was sitting quietly across from his challenging seven-year-old daughter at a casual hamburger restaurant, when he took a packet of sugar, opened it, and sprinkled it all over his daughter. She was flabbergasted. He was just acting silly. He then proceeded to throw a french fry on her head. She retaliated and then giggled with delight. Of course it did take a bit to stop the food fight, but it was worth it. Renee talked about the incident for weeks. Her friends were fascinated by tales of her food fight with her daddy.

Once in a while, it's OK to join the ranks of the challengers. Let loose. Do the unexpected. It is important for your child to see another side of you.

Janice took a hip-hop class at the same dance studio as her 10-year-old daughter, Gail. Gail was aghast. "What's my mom doing here dancing hip-hop?!" But then as she saw how much fun Janice was having, she began to enjoy seeing her mom enjoy herself. They even made up hip-hop routines together.

You need to be on your challenger's side. This is often accomplished by engaging in activities that are fun and active like dance, sports, music, and art.

Your child, wanting to participate in these activities with you, will be more apt to cooperate. But don't threaten to take away these fun activities as a form of punishment. Keep your special times together just that—special.

BEING RAISED RIGHT

On a train ride from Baltimore to Washington, D.C., I struck up a conversation with a woman knitting a sweater for her niece's birthday. She asked me what I did. I explained my background as a child and family psychologist to which she sharply replied, "The *only* family psychology we had in our house was the notion that if you were an O'Connell everyone knew you were raised right." I asked to her explain . . . and explain she did:

"We were taught that there was an O'Connell way of doing things. We all pitched in on chores, and the fact that the Riley kids stayed up to 11 o'clock had nothing to do with what the O'Connell kids did. If one of us kids had a problem we all worked to solve it. Just like the Three Musketeers: 'One for all and all for one!' At times it was hard because there was this standard to live up to—but I knew who I was, where I belonged, and who I would have to answer to when I did something bad."

As I came to understand, during that sixty minute ride to D.C., "being raised right" was a set of values, goals, attitudes, and behaviors that each member of the family was expected to live by and adhere to. Peer pressure or other outside demands seemed less important in face of these values. "Being raised right" instills the idea that everyone's needs in the family must be met, not just one individual's. Moreover, in my work with challenging children, these values help provide a structure or safety net which helps them remain focused and positive. "Being raised right" also helps challengers become less manipulative because they become concerned with working together and sharing.

It may sound, at times, like an idea from a fifties television show, but in light of so many family pressures and demands "being raised right" seems like a smart way to raise *any* child—especially a challenger.

3

Discipline That Diffuses Conflict

NEGOTIATING FOR SUCCESS

If ever there was a subject close to a challenged parent's heart, it is discipline. As a parent of a challenger you probably feel like all you do is discipline your child. It's often a day-to-day routine of conflict, fights, anger, and power struggles. Challengers keep us in the "ready mode"—ready for action. There rarely seems to be a relaxed time. You fantasize about the moment that you will say to your child, "Please pick up your toys," and he will respond happily, "Okay, sure, right away."

Those words of agreement are not well-known to a challenged parent who has come to expect a groan, an excuse, or a negotiation. Perhaps, unconsciously or consciously, you have labeled your challenger, "obstinate, defiant, and difficult." Children begin to believe they are these things because they intrinsically believe in us and what we say. But it is important that you believe in your child because the real purpose of discipline is to convey love and teach responsibility.

It is also important to *stop placing unrealistic expectations* on your child because you have an agenda you want to complete. Challengers have their own unique agenda. Try to explore your child's inner world so that you can understand his motivations better. By doing so, you will validate your child's feelings and ultimately build self-esteem.

Remember the girl who created an incredible Barbie world all over her room? Her mom wanted it cleaned up. The daughter begged her to let her keep it. Instead of getting into a power struggle, this mom was able to see things from her daughter's perspective. She said, "I see you have built a beautiful Barbie city. I'll let you keep it up for a few more days, and then let's clean it up together, and you can create a new city over the weekend."

Fair negotiation will help avoid fights. Instead of creating a power struggle with your child, be willing to negotiate and see his point of view. How would you like it if you worked on a crossword puzzle and had three words to finish, but someone threw the paper away in order to clean up the mess?

A parent often responds to his challenger by imposing more limits as a way to short circuit the child's demands. It's as if the antidote to a challenger's constant demands is increasingly stiff parental limits. A negotiating style with challengers is essential. But before you negotiate, you have to be clear about the risks involved.

When your child wants to negotiate something, it is important to do a family risk assessment first, which takes into consideration the health, safety, and values of your child and family.

Risk Assessment

Health Ask yourself if there is any danger or risk to your child's health. Determine what is negotiable and what is not. For instance, would a particular food cause allergies, cavities, or exacerbate an illness? Is the activity contrary to your beliefs in raising a healthy child? For instance, if your diabetic child asked to eat a bag of candy she received as a present, then that is a high health risk and becomes a nonnegotiable item. Sugar-free candy is an alternative.

Safety Is there a risk or danger to your child or others? Some safety risks are nonnegotiable like allowing your child to ride without a seat belt or crossing a busy intersection by himself. On the other hand, some parents may allow their child to microwave popcorn without supervision. Others may feel that is non-negotiable and too risky.

Values

Personal Assess your personal, religious, or spiritual beliefs. Does your child's request go against these? Does it invade personal privacy? For instance, would you allow your child to watch MTV, or take some sips of wine, or enter a bedroom without knocking?

Family This entails evaluating chores and responsibilities that most families share. If your child complained that he didn't want to do chores, would you allow him to not do them? Perhaps it would be better to negotiate **trades** and

compromises. For example, tell him you would be willing to do the dishes as a trade-off if he would take out the trash. Each family member has to decide what is negotiable and non-negotiable.

DIFFUSING CONFLICTS

You will not need a long, detailed chart to tell you if you have a challenging child. You'll know it.

If you did have a parent "feeling" chart it might read something like:

- ☐ Exhausted
- ☐ Exasperated
- ☐ Frustrated
- ☐ Elated
- ☐ Confused
- ☐ Feeling ambiguous
- ☐ Nervous

If you checked off at least four or more of the above traits, chances are you are a challenged parent and face conflict with your child on a daily basis.

You came into this life with every intention of being a wonderful parent. You've read every book, bought every video, researched every magazine, and swore you wouldn't repeat the mistakes your parents made. So why do you have such a challenging child? What did you do wrong? Chances are, nothing. There are no perfect parents—or children.

Challengers require special parenting skills that you may

not have prepared for. The most important thing to remember is that challengers don't suddenly change and become quiet, docile children. They are unique children—often high-spirited and utterly delightful. Don't try to push your child into a mold—you'll only create further frustration for yourself and him.

Respect your child's specialness, and learn everything you can about your challenging child because you'll need a well equipped "parents' arsenal of tools" for diffusing conflict.

Communication Skills

Before you begin any family interaction, it is important to have some basic communication skills that will help you to approach your child positively so that you can diffuse conflicts in a reasonable way. These skills will also help you and your child communicate in a clear and concise manner.

- Sit down with your child at eye level.
- Really listen. Don't let the phone or other distractions divert your attention.
- Make direct eye contact.
- Ask open-ended questions like, "I don't understand why you're fighting with your sister. Let's talk about it."
- Mirroring reflects back what the child is feeling and lets him feel understood. Use it as a way to validate a child's feelings while continuing to set a limit. For example, you might say, "I know you would love to eat these chocolate cookies before dinner, but it is not OK."
- Make specific requests. Rather than saying, "Clean up

your room," say, "Clean the toys from under the bed and put away your books."

- Ask your child to repeat his understanding of your request.
- Separate your child's behavior from how you view him personally. Avoid saying, "You're bad for not listening to me." Instead say, "Your *behavior* was not acceptable. I feel upset when you don't listen to my request to clean the fish tank."
- Avoid empty threats. Be careful of using words like "always" and "never." If you say, "I will never let you ride your bicycle again," chances are you don't really mean it, and your child will not take your threats seriously.
- Make "I" statements. "I" statements avoid direct accusations. Say, "I really wish you would listen better when I speak to you," instead of, "You never listen when I talk to you." Be less accusatory and antagonistic.
- Express love often and admit mistakes. If you can say you're sorry and show forgiveness, then your child will learn to model this behavior.

Equal Consideration

In order to avoid conflicts, you have to be willing to give your child equal time and equal consideration. Equal consideration is the notion that you will listen to what your child has to say, and you will consider his thoughts and feelings even though you may not acquiesce to his request. But equal treatment focuses ultimately on you as a parent and your willingness to express the idea that you will make the ultimate decision and do what's best for your child. For example, you will consider your 11-year-old son's request to stay up until 11:00 p.m. However, because your 16-year-old daughter stays up until 11:00 p.m. is not a reason to extend your son's bedtime. Your son should expect equal consideration, not equal treatment.

You should evaluate all points of view, but you make the decisions, regarding matters of health, safety, and house rules.

Use some of the following techniques:

- **Validate** your child's feelings by saying, "You are so good at being persistent. That's a great skill. I know you want to stay up late, but the answer is still, 'No!' "
- **Empathize** with how your child is seeing and feeling about things. Put yourself in his mind. Tell him you understand how it feels to be disappointed.

It is important to create a partnership with your child. This parent/child partnership is based on equal consideration—not equal treatment. Being an effective parent is not necessarily about equality.

Fair Family Meeting

In an attempt to guide your challenger for preparation in the real world, it is important to teach him to listen and relate to others. This can be accomplished by creating the "fair family meeting" which helps to further promote equal consideration.

The fair family meeting is just that—a meeting where the family gets to work together on solutions to a problem without yelling, blame, or criticism. It can help teach your child to listen more effectively and enhances his verbal and analytical skills.

The fair family meeting brings together all of the family members to discuss a particular problem or topic. Each family member gets between two to five minutes (depending on age and the attention span of the child) to discuss his or her point of view. No one can interrupt. This exercise gives equal time and equal consideration to each person. The meeting also allows you to give complete attention to your child without making a judgment.

The fair family meeting is an excellent problem-solving model for children. It averts frustrating corners which challengers often back themselves into.

Guidelines for a Fair Family Meeting

- Make an appointment to meet.
- Cover a specific topic.
- Use a timer to keep the meeting focused. When the timer rings, the meeting is over.
- "Mirror" your child's feelings by saying, "I understand you want to stay up as late as your sister."
- Feel okay about leaving the topic unresolved. In fact, don't expect to resolve problems in one meeting. You are trying to create an open forum for your family.
- Set a future time to continue discussing the topic until a resolution or a consensus is reached.

Use the family meeting as a teaching tool and let it help you learn more about how your child organizes the world.

Problem Solving

Problem solving not only diffuses conflict but also teaches responsibility. A child's ability to resolve problems empowers him to feel in control. Challengers especially have trouble problem solving because they tend to be impulsive. The following steps will diminish anxiety and escalation and promote conflict resolution.

Problem Solving Steps:

- Talk about your child's feelings. Ask what's bothering her. Say, "You look sad. What's going on?"
- Let your child know that problems are solvable. Explain how you have solved some of your own.
- Brainstorm. Think of all the possibilities for solving the problem and find a mutually agreeable solution.
- Write down the ideas without evaluation. For instance, let's say your child forgot her homework at school. Some ideas for solving the problem are:

    1. If school is still open, go back for it and ask the janitor to open the room if it is locked.
    2. Call a friend and get the homework assignment.
    3. Call the teacher.
    4. Explain to your teacher that you forgot it, and ask if you can make it up on another day.

- Decide which suggestions you like, which ones you don't like, and which ones you plan to follow through on.

- Have faith—faith is an attitude, like cheerleading, which indicates by facial expression, tone of voice, and actions, that we believe a solution to the problem can be found. It is an attitude of hope which leaves children feeling supported and positive.

Time-Out

Time-out is an effective tool that can be used when kids act out physically and emotionally. Time-outs are a way of keeping conflict from getting out of hand (with yelling and hitting). You remove your child and place him in a quiet, non-stimulating area. Time-outs are for children but can help parents get a hold of themselves as well. Time-outs can especially serve the challenging child because of the challenger's propensity for escalating.

If you wait too long before implementing a time-out, it's too late. Once a child is in a full-force tantrum or escalating beyond reason, a time-out may not work.

Parent Plan

- Be consistent and use time-outs after only one warning. If you give continual threats, your child will not listen or take your warnings seriously.
- Make sure you stay calm. If you are yelling, your challenger will too.
- Give a time-out in a neutral place. No bedrooms or playrooms where there are too many "fun" distractions. A hallway often works best.

- Put the child on a chair, and set the timer (one minute for each year of his age).
- Time-out is a springboard for an interaction with your child at a later date. You want to help your child put his feelings into words. After the time-out, you can talk to your child in a calm manner.

When you use a time-out, it helps to ask your child afterwards, "What would have been another way to act? What could you have done differently?"

THE 4 Cs

The 4 Cs create a framework for your family to set clear limits and further diffuse conflicts on a day-to-day basis.

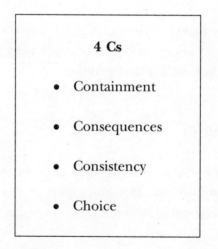

4 Cs

- Containment
- Consequences
- Consistency
- Choice

Perfect Results

The 4 Cs need to be used altogether. Just like you can't bake chocolate cookies without sugar, flour, and chocolate chips, likewise, you need to follow through with the 4 Cs in order to achieve positive results. The 4 Cs minimizes your child's feeling personally attacked by focusing on his behavior.

In order for us to be successful parents, the methods of diffusing conflicts and setting limits must work together. The more your child struggles to take responsibility for his actions, the more you can help him problem solve. The more consistent you are, the more likely your child will learn about self-discipline and responsibility. In that way, he will see discipline as an act of love and one in which he can participate.

Conflict arises when discipline is perceived as punishment or an impulsive response to a behavior rather than a logical and/or natural consequence of his action. The child's self-esteem diminishes when a parent is out of control. Children feel safe and flourish in a world that is predictable and dependable.

The limit-setting devices of the 4 Cs—containment, consequences, consistency, and choice—will help you and your challenger negotiate and compromise.

CONTAINMENT

Containment sets limits on your child's behavior. A child feels safe when he knows that his parents set reasonable limits. Without boundaries, a challenger feels out of control, because he often doesn't think about the consequences of his behavior. If he doesn't have a limit, he won't stop inappropriate actions.

Parent Plan

- Do not set limits in the heat of battle.
- You must discuss in advance specific behavior you want to work with.
- Explain why you are doing what you are doing. For instance say, "I want you to go to bed at 8:00. Your teachers are letting me know you seem tired, and it shows in your work."
- Whether your child agrees or not, those are reasonable expectations. Express your request in a broken record manner with a neutral voice and repeat it as often as necessary.
- Assess your request. Make sure it feels fair. For instance, you're not asking your child to go to bed at 5:00. You are making a compromise and a reasonable one by asking him to go to bed at 8:00.
- Teach your children how to use language to reach a goal. Challengers tend to act out verbally and escalate emotionally. When you teach your child how to use language in a thoughtful way, it models more appropriate (contained) behavior. For example, "Seth, your voice is too loud. We'll continue to discuss this when your tone is quieter."

CONSEQUENCES

Consequences teach responsibility. The more your child is responsible for her behavior, the greater her self-esteem.

Some "natural consequences" can be excellent teaching devices. For example, let's say it's cold outside. You beg your child to take a sweater to school. He refuses and starts to escalate. So you let him go without a sweater. After school, he says he was freezing all morning. Then he gets a cold, and can't go to the movies with his friends. The next week, he decides on his own to bring a sweater without your having to ask.

Parents often use logical consequences (no TV unless you finish your homework) to avert natural consequences (a D in math). Natural consequences and logical consequences help children to see the world in an organized way. Of course, natural consequences are only valid after a risk assessment has been done. We don't want our children learning about the danger of playing in the street by getting hit by a car.

CONSISTENCY

Challengers will sometimes push limits just to see if parents will impose consequences. If you set rules, then you have to be willing to enforce those rules to increase parental credibility. Do not set limits or consequences if you can't follow through or have someone else follow through.

The ability to be consistent helps children succeed as well as express love and caring. Consistency helps a child feel secure. He knows what is expected—all the time. By being consistent, your child will learn the 4th C: choice.

CHOICE

Choice helps your child achieve *self-control.* You are asking him to make a choice by deciding how he will behave in a certain situation.

In the following situation Nick wants to play Nintendo, but his mother wants him to take a bath. Therefore, she can frame a choice: "You can play Nintendo for five minutes now and then take a bath *or* you can have your bath now and play Nintendo for fifteen minutes later."

The child is not being threatened. He is asked to make a simple choice. Ultimately this teaches responsibility. If he makes the choice for an early bath, he receives the consequences—more Nintendo. He becomes responsible for the choice and the consequence.

It is important for Nick's mother to emphasize ahead of time that it is *his* choice when to play Nintendo. Remember, if your child does not do what you ask, and if you are not willing to put up with his choice then don't set that up as a choice.

Choices teach self-control and responsibility and allow a child to learn that there are consequences to his behavior. A child who takes responsibility for actions is well-liked because he is less likely to blame others when something goes wrong. He also knows how to compromise. These concepts help build a strong sense of self-esteem, which is especially important for a challenging child.

MA AND PA

There are two ways of making the 4 Cs even more successful: "ma" and "pa."

MA = **More Approval.** Look for ways to compliment what your child does. Catch her being "good."

PA = **Praising Approximations.** Acknowledge the "little steps" that your child has made toward gradual improvement and achievement of goals.

When 10-year-old Todd's mom asked him to clean up his room, he was hesitant but managed to put away a few toys. The room still looked messy, but Gloria used PA, and praised his effort when he put *some* of his toys away.

She said, "I know it's easy to get distracted when you clean your room, but I'm glad you got started and were able to put some of your toys away. Next time, work on putting more Lego's away."

Because of the competitive nature of a challenger, he might be unwilling to take on a task if he doesn't think he can do well. This is where MA and PA help. These techniques can boost a child's self-esteem by helping him reach goals successfully. MA and PA teach your child that you appreciate what he *does* do, not what he *doesn't* do, and that you value the small steps he is taking to achieve a goal.

Places Where MA and PA Can Work Effectively

- MA (more approval) This should have no contingencies, no "hitches." Appreciate what your child has done, not what he hasn't.

  Resist the impulse to "get everything in" with your

child at once. Because of this, you may confuse your child with your requests and undermine the good feelings that come from praise. Sometimes parents have a tendency to give conditional praise. If you say to your child, "Gee, you got a good report card," and then go on to qualify your praise by saying, "Next time you could do even better," you have immediately negated the value of more approval (MA).

This mixed message may teach your child that the real reason for your approval was to make another demand. Inevitably, this approach will diminish his motivation to do well. Accept what he has done and choose another time to discuss other areas that need improvement.

- PA (praising approximations) Choose *one* aspect of what your child has done and work to improve it, but always focus on the small incremental ways he can accomplish this goal. Don't flood your child with everything that he needs to do the next time he cleans up. It becomes overwhelming. Raise one issue at a time. Always praise his efforts.

These techniques are an attempt to accept the child as is—not always an easy task, but ultimately a rewarding one.

TANTRUMS

Challengers often have escalating episodes that may lead to tantrums. In the simplest terms, tantrums are a cry for attention. *The extent to which parents do not respond to tantrums is the degree to which kids stop this behavior.*

Let's explain this idea further. If your child is having a tantrum (as long as he is not hurting himself), withdraw from the situation and say in a calm manner, "When you're done with your tantrum, we'll talk about it."

Do not worry about the neighbors if your child gets loud, because believe it or not, most people will identify with you.

Do not put your child in a situation he can't handle, like a busy mall at 5:00 p.m. when he's tired, hungry, and cranky. Try not to push a challenging child beyond his limits.

However, if you find yourself in a public place with a tantruming child, the simplest solution is to remove yourselves from the situation. If you're in the market with a basketful of groceries, leave them. Go to your car. If your child continues to tantrum, say to him, as above, "I'm going to wait outside while you're screaming. When you're done, I'll come back into the car and we can talk about it."

PREDICTABILITY OF BEHAVIOR

A challenger's behavior is fairly predictable. One mom put her challenger to bed hoping she would go right to sleep. Suddenly an hour later the child is still up asking for water, a back rub, and a song. With a challenger, it is likely that the same things happen over and over again. It's up to you to decide ahead of time how to deal with such repetitive behavior.

You'll have to contain your unrealistic expectations and learn to accept your challenger. If you know that your child will whine and complain every time you take him to the grocery store, then don't take him unless you have a strategy. Discuss his behavior ahead of time and make a contract between the two of you. "I have to take you with me. I know you don't like the grocery store, but maybe after we shop for an hour, we can do something you would like. What would you like to do?"

These predictable repetitive behaviors do not change overnight. It takes a real conscious effort of applying the 4 Cs on a day-to-day basis for change to occur.

SAYING WHAT YOU MEAN, MEANING WHAT YOU SAY

Behaviour changes when you consistently "say what you mean and mean what you say." Avoiding idle threats like, "I'll never take you to the park again...," helps your child know that the limits you set are reasonable and enforceable.

SET YOUR PRIORITIES

Set your priorities and decide what is really worth making an issue about. Perhaps this is the most important thing to remember about disciplining a challenger.

Parent Plan

- Choose your fights and your battles. Many things are not that important. Otherwise, kids tune you out and don't listen.

- Only deal with high-priority issues. Make a list of what you think are the 10 highest priorities in your family for your school age child. Ask your child to do the same.
- Be consistent about appropriate expectations and limits. Your kids will feel safer when you are.
- Give your children choices within reasonable boundaries.
- Follow through on agreements.
- Focus on and praise the good behaviors and what your child does well.
- Admit when you've made a mistake.

Disciplining your challenging child does not have to become a war. By using the methods outlined in this chapter, you will be able to adopt a parental plan of action based on mutual respect and communication. These are the key tools in diffusing conflicts.

4

The Family Challenge

COMING OUT OF CHILDHOOD

Coming out of childhood is a lifelong process. How well we succeed and guide our children through childhood depends on how well we have explored our own feelings. You may face many challenges in understanding your responses to your child's actions. Remember, while you are trying to work through and raise your children, you are also attempting to grow and enlighten yourself.

Having a challenging child can leave you so frustrated that you feel all the good work you try to do falls apart with one hysterical outburst. You may live with the hope that he will somehow change into a different kind of child as time passes. This is often not the case. The reality is your child will grow and change and most likely continue to pose a challenge to you, and believe it or not, you may pose a challenge to your child.

The family interaction is important to understand, to work on together, and to change, if necessary. The reactions your child evokes from others often impact your sense of who you are as a parent and a person. Sadly, you may even feel like giving up on your child by the time he is a teenager because you could not understand his reactions early on.

When Michael became an adult, he told his parents that when he was growing up, he felt like the "black sheep" in the family. Since he knew he was always getting into trouble, he felt ostracized. On the other hand, Michael's parents felt they gave him more attention than his brother because of his challenging nature, but were at a loss to help him understand their reactions to him.

Michael was labeled a "problem" early on and as a result his family seemed to expect bad behavior from him. We often live out the labels we receive—the rebel, the nerd, the brain, the bad boy, the sweet thing. Often the biggest challenge you may face is to deal with your children as individuals and not members of a category. Address your child's individual needs after a thoughtful assessment of whom your child really is. Remember, even if your challenger has different abilities and ways of looking at the world, so do we all.

The following chart will give you an idea of what often occurs between a parent and a challenging child. This will help you understand yourself, so that you can better help him. Let's take an everyday example of a child cleaning his room:

Parent Request	Child Response	Parent Internal Response
"Please clean up your room."	Doesn't answer.	Wishes child will obey.
Louder, "Pick up your clothes. I'm not going to ask again."	"Later!"	Parent(s) feel(s) their authority is being challenged.

Parent Request	Child Response	Parent Internal Response
Yells, "Now!"	Whining. "Stop it, Mom! Why are you yelling at me?"	Parent feels wounded.
Parent grabs child by arm. "No T.V. tonight. You're grounded."	Child gets hysterical. Screams, rants, out of control.	Parent feels out of control.
Loses control, screams, "Pick up your clothes."	Child yells, screams at parent, "Stop. I hate you."	Parent feels attacked and feels like a bad parent.

The previous sequence gives you an idea of what goes on internally in a parent/child power struggle. Your guilt and anger may give you a clue that something deeper needs to be explored, something that may be about your own childhood experiences. The purpose of this chart and explanation is to give you a better understanding of how a simple situation can escalate. You do have alternative responses and your awareness can break this cycle of conflict with your challenging child.

PARENTAL RESPONSE

How could such a commonplace occurrence as asking your child to clean up his room lead to such a conflict? Let's explore what really happened between you and your child.

What Happens Psychologically

In asking your child to clean up his room, you perceive yourself as making a reasonable request. Your hidden agenda may be that you want to perceive yourself as a good parent. The conflict is unconscious. You may be thinking, "If my child listens (cleans his room), then I am a good parent." There is an underlying need that you are seeking to fulfill. For some parents, it is reassurance that their child is well-mannered. A child's compliance is equated with being a good parent. For other parents, compliance is equated with love or respect. A parent of a challenging child will find it difficult to receive this type of validation. The real issue may not be about cleaning up the room.

- When your child responds by ignoring you, you may perceive it as a threat to your success, your value as a parent.
- Examine your own experiences growing up. Ask yourself the following questions: Where does it come from that my child's actions are equated with being a good parent? What happened if I didn't listen to my parents? Would I get punished and yelled at? Could my child be doing something I could never do, like asserting my own opinions and thoughts?
- Your child may hear in your tone of voice and body language criticism and judgment, which make it nearly impossible to respond to your request.
- Both of you fear that you are "not good enough." Your feelings of guilt may come from the knowledge that whatever your request and your child's response were, they did not warrant such a strong reaction. This may feel like a repetition of your experiences as a child. For his part, your child may feel inadequate and misunderstood.

Why Do Some Parents Feel Wounded?

- You may sometimes feel devalued when your child disobeys. This internal feeling of being hurt can rekindle an old wound from your own childhood, if your parents didn't listen to or value you.
- When you lose control, the unconscious reaction toward your child may be "I'm upset with you for bringing up these old feelings."

BREAKING THE CYCLE OF CONFLICT

Challenging kids often bring out our unconscious feelings. The struggle is to separate your child's actions from your perception of yourself as a parent. This is not an easy task. As we have explained some of the conflict between you and your child is a repeat of what happened to you as a child.

An important clue that the conflict is an unconscious repeat of the past is that you may get locked into a power struggle that is not entirely about the original request. You need to become aware of your hidden agenda in order to relate properly to your child.

Let's look at what would be a corrected internal response to the problem of room cleaning.

PARENT RESPONSE CHART

Parent Request	Child Response	Parent Internal Response	Corrective Internal Response
Please clean up your room.	Doesn't answer.	Wishes child will obey.	**Do not personalize child's response. It's not about the parent.**
Louder. "Pick up your clothes. I'm not going to ask again."	"Later!"	Parent(s) feel(s) their authority is being challenged.	**Parents have to ask themselves, "Is my daughter challenging my authority by saying, 'Later?' "**
Yells, "Now!"	Whining. "Stop it, Mom! Why are you yelling at me?"	Parent feels wounded.	**Ask child, "Is there a reason why you did not listen?" Parents have to ask themselves why they feel wounded.**
Parent grabs child by arm. "No T.V. tonight. You're grounded."	Child gets hysterical. Screams, rants, out of control.	Parent feels out of control.	**I feel out of control, and I know my child is out of control. We need to break this now and talk later. "Time-out. We need a break from each other."**
Loses control, screams, "Pick up your clothes."	Child yells, screams at parent, "Stop. I hate you."	Parent feels attacked and feels like a bad parent.	**This has gone too far. It's only about picking up clothes. "I love you."**

Marcia is constantly struggling to get her five-year-old son, Nicholas, to eat his vegetables, but he absolutely refuses. She's tried everything, to no avail. At some point she gives up the struggle, but she's angry. She perceives herself as being a bad parent because she thinks that she is not giving her child the proper nutrition. This is compounded by Nicholas's unwillingness to listen to what she believes to be important. Now, Marcia feels guilty and angry at Nicholas for not listening. He is confused by her extreme reaction. Nicholas becomes angry as well and he starts to escalate.

When we are in the midst of conflict with a challenging child, we often lose sight of what we want to accomplish. By breaking down our internal thoughts and feelings, we can often diminish conflict simply by de-escalating and by refocusing on what's important. Corrected parental responses will help your child with his reactions by modeling more appropriate behavior.

The following chart shows another example of the parent/child responses to family turmoil and an appropriate corrective parent response. You can use the blank chart on page 81 with your own child.

PARENT RESPONSE CHART

Parent Request	Child Response	Parent Internal Response	Corrective Internal Response
"Please eat your vegetables."	"I don't like vegetables."	How am I going to get him to eat his veggies?	**Parent asks himself, "Why is it so important that he eats his vegetables?"**
"Just take a few bites."	"No!"	What's wrong with me? I can never get him to even take a bite.	**I'm personalizing because he's not eating his veggies.**
Parent is angry. "I said, eat them!"	"I hate them!" Starts to cry.	Parent feels hopeless, out of control.	**Eating vegetables is not worth this fighting.**
"There is no choice. You have to eat them. They're good for you!"	Child knocks vegetables on the floor.	Parent feels like a failure and guilty.	**Let's find a solution to this problem. Say, "I love you. You're more important to me than vegetables."**

PARENT RESPONSE CHART

Parent Request	Child Response	Parent Internal Response	Corrective Internal Response

THE "UNEXPRESSED FELT"

The "unexpressed felt" has a double meaning. First, it relates to your child's ability to express feelings or thoughts that you may be avoiding. Secondly, children tend to act out the tensions and struggles that occur in the family.

Children are sensitive. They read in our tone and body language what we are feeling. Consequently, they react to those feelings although they are not verbalized.

Alexandra's parents were having financial problems. They walked around moody, depressed, and short-tempered. Alexandra was more overt. She started throwing her toys all over her room. She whined and was loud. Her parents became furious at her. Their punishing her only escalated the situation. In reality, however, Alexandra was acting out the constant tension and anxiety her parents were displaying for weeks in the home. She needed an emotional outlet as well, but didn't know how else to get her needs met.

The anger we display toward our spouses and others is easily picked up by our children who act out in ways we may perceive as bad behavior. In actuality, however, your child may be expressing your feelings through her actions. Try to put into words your own feelings by having fair family meetings often during stressful times. This will help your child become less anxious and less likely to act out.

SIBLING CHALLENGE

Challengers often take center stage in a family. This is difficult if you are struggling to meet other children's needs. This creates another challenge for you.

For example, some challengers may not read social cues well. They may not read body language or facial expressions well and are therefore perceived as demanding and aggressive toward their siblings.

If the older child, a challenger, is left to baby-sit a younger sibling, there can be lots of shouting and controlling behavior that might sound like, "I told you to go to bed. Why aren't you listening to me? You have to do what I say."

If the younger sibling is the challenger, and is being baby-sat by an older sibling, the challenger will be defiant and oppositional, and probably refuse to go to bed.

You must weigh your options: Do you allow your challenger to be in charge? What rules do you establish? Should you get an adult baby-sitter to take over the responsibility? How much disciplining, if any, is an older sibling permitted to use on a younger challenging sibling?

Besides the negative interactions that can occur between siblings, there is often the problem of the unchallenging sibling being left to fend for herself. This leaves the parent with another dilemma: how to respond to the "quieter" child.

For example, challenger John, 14, had a sister Rita, 11. Rita didn't want to trouble her parents with her needs because John was so difficult. She was determined to become the really "good girl." She rarely brought up her own problems, or talked about what she was doing in school, or her friends. Rita did not communicate much at all. She reacted by withdrawing from the family and her brother. Her parents were not even aware of Rita's feelings, because they were so used to her being the quiet, compliant child.

Siblings sometimes do not have a relationship with a brother or sister who is challenging. They don't want to have anything to do with him or her. Also, parents may put all their focus on the challenging child. They give a lot of praise and overcompensate for their challenger, while the sibling feels shunned.

You may think the sibling will understand the family dynamic simply because she does not complain. You are so appreciative of her easy manner that you may ignore her needs.

Some siblings will excel in areas completely different from their challenging sibling on purpose. For example, Rita's parents misinterpreted her avoiding playing the violin as disinterest, when in actuality she chose not to take up the instrument because she didn't want to be in competition with John's playing. She already excelled in the guitar.

You need to help encourage your child to excel in areas she wants to. Even if John didn't like Rita's playing the violin, her family needed to give her support.

Sometimes the unchallenging sibling adopts behaviors opposite to that of the challenger. Ten-year-old Gena, for example, became obsessed about her bookcase. Every book had to be lined up perfectly, every author had to be alphabetical, and the hardcovers and softcovers had to be separated. If one book was out of place, she became upset.

Conversely, her challenging brother, Scott, could care less about his books or his room. It was always a mess. Ironically, the messier Scott's room got, the neater Gena's became. The more trouble Scott got into for not putting his books away, the more focused Gena became on keeping her bookcase neat. She was determined to do everything completely opposite of her challenging brother.

In order for Gena's parents to be effective, it is necessary for them to wonder, "Why is Gena getting so focused on her bookcase being perfect? What's going on with Gena?" When Gena's parents asked these questions they learned that she needed to feel in control and was frustrated with her brother.

You may face recognizing that there is a ripple effect on

other siblings' feelings in dealing with your challenging child. Use the following parental plan to help work through challenger/sibling interactions.

Parent Plan

- Have family meetings. Encourage your children to talk to one another about their feelings.
- Take one issue, like the bookcase, and ask a question such as, "How can the family help you understand that our love is not based on how clean or messy either of your rooms is. Have we given you that message?"

Pay attention to each child's unique needs, even if they go unexpressed.

FAMILY INTERACTIONS

Other family members—grandparents, aunts, uncles, cousins—are often critical of how you raise your children. However well-meaning, a constant barrage of suggestions tells families with challengers that they are doing it wrong. Ultimately, parents feel defensive and sometimes avoid family interactions and outings.

Betty recalls her mother-in-law remarking, "I don't understand how anyone can handle your unruly son." Grandma suggested that perhaps Betty was not feeding her grandson properly or getting him to sleep early enough.

Betty was hurt and angry at these remarks. She became

defensive. Every time Derek was supposed to see Grandma, she would get anxious and lecture him about all the things he shouldn't do. Subsequently, Derek became anxious as well. What was supposed to be a fun time turned into an unhappy experience.

A parent often feels guilty and ashamed when others impugn their parenting. There is this constant self-examination and questioning: What am I doing wrong? These feelings run deep, especially when you have tried everything, and are left to face the judgment of others.

You should not have to defend yourself. Parties and family gatherings can be a source of tension for you as well your kids. Therefore, it is necessary to prepare yourself, your child, and family members before conflict occurs.

Parent Plan

Take a pro-active, problem-solving, strategizing position.

- Avoid putting your child in a situation where you know he'll feel uncomfortable and act out.
- Prepare other family members in advance. Explain to your family members or friends. "Nick gets rowdy in social situations, and he may need some time alone so he can regain self-control."
- When possible, limit the event to two to three hours or less, if necessary. It can be too much for a challenging child to be at a party too long. Challengers can get over-stimulated.
- Transitions are difficult. Some kids have trouble leaving,

and the family needs to know how you are going to deal with leaving. Grandparents can help by saying, "Okay, it's time to go. Let's help you pack things up. We'll do it together."

- Parents need to talk to their challenger. At a family meeting say, "We know you have trouble leaving, so we'll tell you fifteen minutes in advance so you can get ready to go."
- If possible limit people at parties if that causes too much stimulation. By following this plan, parents will ease tensions.
- Remember, your goal is for everyone to have a good time.

CHALLENGE FOR TWO-CAREER FAMILIES

For the parents of a challenging child, it is even more difficult when both parents are working. A challenger has trouble delaying his wants, and immediately bombards his parents the minute they walk in the door. He doesn't understand it when you say, "I'm tired. I need time alone," or "Wait until I'm finished with my work."

A major struggle for working parents is that boundaries and limits often get pushed back. This specifically impacts challengers who need clear boundaries. Parents become less consistent, and the structure falls apart.

As you can imagine, if five-year-old Susie resists taking her bath and eating dinner until you both get home at 7 p.m., it causes a great deal of frustration and chaos, when you walk in the door.

Susie is whiny, the baby-sitter is upset, and you both have to jump into the fray the minute you arrive home.

You may feel tempted to change the rules just this once, to stop the hassles, but that would create unclear boundaries for Susie. All of you need safe and familiar limits, yet because of your own needs, you may find yourselves being inconsistent. The result is that Susie doesn't fully believe that there are limits and will push even harder the next time.

Parent Plan

- Become a united front. Let Susie know that you will back up each others' decisions.
- Strategize in advance how you will deal with Susie if she has not complied with the caretaker's requests.
- Plan special time when you can give her your full attention.
- Utilize problem solving methods discussed in Chapter 3.

George's teacher calls you to say that George is falling asleep in class. You have not set clear boundaries about bedtime because you want to spend time with him when you get home from work. As a result, George's bedtime is getting later and later, and it is starting to affect his school work.

There has to be a specific structure set up for your child when you are at work. He needs to know what his limits are, even when you are not there. Create a schedule on a chart and be consistent every day about having him and the baby-sitter follow the time frame. The times may change, but a basic framework can help organize your child's day while you are at work. Perhaps you would consider devising a chart like the following:

Afterschool Schedule

Mon.	Snack 3:00	Homework 3:30–4:30	Play 4:30–5:30	Bath 5:30–6:00	Dinner 6:30	Story 7:30	Bed 8:00
Tues.	Snack 3:30	Soccer Practice 4:00–5:00	Homework 5:30–6:00	Dinner 6:00	Bath 7:00	Story 7:30	Bed 8:30
Wed.	Snack	Homework	Play	Bath	Dinner	Story	Bed
Thurs.	Snack	Gymnastics	Homework/ Play	Bath	Dinner	Story	Bed
Fri.	Snack	Homework	Play Date	Bath	Dinner	Story	Bed

Afterschool Schedule

Mon.							
Tues.							
Wed.							
Thurs.							
Fri.							

Obviously, every family will have a different schedule. Your child might have a birthday party, or a doctor's appointment, but, a basic schedule should be followed as much as possible. These schedules will help the whole family because they will help your challenger know exactly what to do and when.

I'm sure you're wondering what happens if the schedule

is not followed. Clear consequences are necessary in that eventuality. (See Chapter 3.)

You may choose consequences such as limiting television, creating an earlier bed time, or perhaps withholding Nintendo or play dates. Whatever you choose, make sure you or your baby-sitter follow through, and that you are consistent.

You may be faced with a different problem if you work in the home. You are not always available to your child. You need to make it clear that you cannot be interrupted, but will spend "special" time with your child when your work is finished.

Some parents deal with this by taking a 10-minute break every hour. They may put up a sign (red light, green light), which signals when they are ready to interact. The child gets time with his parents that is *all his,* and this interaction can be enriching for both parent and child. Also bear in mind, that when you work in an office you still have interruptions. They are part of the normal work day.

CHALLENGING ONLY CHILDREN

There is so much attention and focus placed on the only child, that parents can lose their perspective, and have difficulty establishing clear boundaries.

Parents of only children can place all of their hopes and dreams on one child. Their desire to create a perfect environment only adds tension to the interactions. Parents become overly worried, attentive, indulgent. The best way to deal with this situation is to pay close attention to limits and boundaries and provide your child with lots of opportunities to interact with others.

THE NECESSARY LOSS

You may feel a loss about having a challenging child. It is a sense that your child is different from others.

You must acknowledge at some point that your child *is* different, and responds to the world uniquely. This is not a judgment about good or bad; it is simply a fact that you need to come to terms with.

In acknowledging your feelings, you may experience some grief. You may keep hoping things will change, but an acknowledgment that your child may always be challenging will inevitably free you to move on to the issues that are most important: building a close relationship, understanding each other, and providing opportunities for your child's success.

Every parent fantasizes about the "perfect" child—sweet, kind, obedient, bright, and creative. But the truth is, no child or human being on Earth is perfect. This fantasy will only frustrate you and especially your child, who can feel your unspoken or spoken disappointment.

It is best to focus on the positive characteristics your child *does* have without comparison to others. Become your child's ally, his protector and caregiver. Let him know how much you love him. Maybe after time, you will not feel a loss at all, but instead you will gain much more than you realized.

TAKING A BREAK

It is okay to want to spend time away from your child. In fact, it is probably a good idea. Challengers can push us beyond our limits, and we make mistakes that hurt the positive strides we have taken. Then we feel guilty and try to over-compensate by giving in.

Sometimes we are feeling burned out, tired, stressed. Our challenger adds one more factor, and we blow up. That's why it is better to walk away from a potentially volatile situation. Confrontation only leads to negative interaction.

If you are overstressed, then spend the evening out. Get a baby-sitter, have your spouse put your child to bed, ask a neighbor to help you out.

Exercise, go for a walk. Spend time with friends. Change your environment and your perspective.

We cannot expect our children to take care of our needs. Therefore, we have to take care of ourselves. Challengers can leave us in tears, frustrated, and totally exasperated. We have to recognize the signals that tell us we've been working too hard and taking on too much.

ACCEPTANCE

Challenged parents often feel inadequate because they are bombarded by so many observations and suggestions for their child—all well intended. Nevertheless, these create the feeling that you are not doing all that you can to help your youngster. In truth, parents of challengers are just as consci-entious, involved, and concerned as parents of non-challeng-ers—in fact even more so. Most parents in this situation try everything to help their child.

Accept yourself and your child.

5

The School Challenge: It's Never Simple

School can often be difficult for an average child, but for a challenger, it can pose many obstacles. Challengers who naturally struggle with boundaries and transitions face huge challenges in school. Boundaries, limits, shaping behavior, and socializing children are a significant part of education, and a challenger who doesn't realize this will constantly experience confusion, anxiety and frustration.

CHILD/TEACHER "MATCH"

When your child matches the teacher's expectations, there is rarely a conflict educationally or behaviorally. However, all students, at one time or the other, encounter a teacher who does not appreciate their inquisitiveness or high-spirited behavior. Challenging children face these problems more often than others.

Perhaps the best way to assure that your child is valued for his uniqueness is to look for a good match. "Match" is analogous to a pair of matching socks—they go together—and there is no question that you need the two together.

It is impossible to create a perfect match with every teacher. For the challenging child, the sense of match with a teacher may be awkward and fleeting. The emotional roller coaster can be wearing on both challengers and teachers because challengers' moods may change frequently, and teachers may lose patience.

As we discussed in Chapter 2, just as there are learning styles, so are there teaching styles. Being able to complement a child's learning style with a teacher's teaching style is the ideal. One teacher may prefer independent work, another may prefer group work. The effectiveness of either teaching style depends upon whether your challenger is introverted or extroverted. (See Chapter 2.) Some teachers are visually oriented, so there is a lot of written material. Some classes are auditorily oriented, so classroom discussions and answering questions aloud are the norm.

There are a number of ways to help your child "match up" with his teacher.

- Parents must become familiar with the child's learning style and be able to communicate that to his teachers. (See Chapter 2.) This is where testing and other methods of diagnosis can be useful if your challenger is having problems. Test results can help the teacher understand any learning difficulties your child may have, and help avoid child/teacher personality conflicts.

- Team work. Parents are often pulled between teacher and child. It is important that a child be a part of the parent/teacher process. Find out if the teacher is receptive to parents being part of the team. Keep in close contact with the teacher about your child's work, behavior, and problems at home.

- When matching child and teacher, parents should ask: 1) Is there a teacher who has structured discipline and is fair to everyone, who has a clear expectation of behavior and performance without favoritism? 2) Does the teacher work well with and understand children with different learning styles? 3) When the teacher realizes the class doesn't understand something, is she willing to try another approach? 4) Is she flexible or does she corner a child by demanding a particular behavior? 5) Is there a teacher whose classroom management style is conducive to a challenging child? Teachers who are consistent, have good follow-through, and a system of consequences with equal treatment for all students are the most conducive for challenging children.

What to Look for in a Teacher

Susan Levine, a Los Angeles-based parent education consultant gives some further ideas on how parents can help choose the best teachers for their challenger:

- It is important to find a teacher who likes to be challenged. Also, remember there is not one "right" kind of teacher.

- You need to know your child's personality and temperament in order to assess which teacher is appropriate for him.
- A parent should try to sit in on classrooms of various teachers.
- Talk to the previous year's teacher about which teacher is best for your youngster.
- Find out from other parents about the teacher's reputation.
- The teacher needs to provide structure, but also creative outlets.
- See how organized the teacher is, that the day is divided in a regular, planned manner, and that the children have clear expectations of the day.

Most important is finding a teacher who values the psychological world of your child and is interested in his feelings and attributes, will take time with your child's anxieties, and is willing to work in partnership with you.

How to Establish a Line of Communication With Your Child's Teacher

As Susan Levine points out, teachers are often overworked and underpaid. They may not have a lot of time for parents. It's important to let the teacher know you are available to hear about your child's progress at the most convenient times for her. If your child does have specific learning difficulties, it is important to collaborate with his teacher and see what you can do to help.

Set up a meeting with the teacher in order to create a match between the home and school learning environment. This will create continuity for the challenged child, which helps him focus on his tasks. Don't be afraid to question the teacher:

- Ask what her expectations are of her students.
- Ask what the homework expectations are.
- Ask how much help the teacher would like you to give your child.
- Would the teacher ever like you to work in the classroom?

Notice what works and what doesn't work for your child. Try to provide activities that are congruent with her learning style.

Nine-year-old Jillian had an important test on the planets. Her mother kept insisting that Jillian study and read over the material. Karen kept asking her to write down the answers. Jillian had trouble focusing. She just couldn't concentrate. When Karen switched to an auditory learning style—orally discussing the material and having her daughter give her the answers verbally—Jillian did much better. In fact, the teacher asked the questions orally, and as a result, Jillian got 100% on the test. (Refer to Chapter 2, the section on Learning Styles.)

Opening up the lines of communication with a teacher can change your child's school life. Don't be afraid to discuss the teacher's teaching style with your child. Explain to your school age child the differences in styles, and how he can better work in his teacher's classroom to make the most of his.

SELF-FULFILLING PROPHECY

Have you ever been in a situation where you were so sure that something bad was going to happen or you were so sure you would fail at a task that it really did happen? These are self-fulfilling prophecies. When we set up a negative thought process toward something, we subconsciously act in a way that will play out the negative consequences we envision.

If you have a preconceived idea about how your challenger acts, and translate your fears to your child's teacher, chances are the teacher will respond to him in a negative way. This plays out your self-fulfilling prophecy: "My challenging child is destined to do poorly."

Ultimately, preconceived attitudes about your child's ability and achievements do impact his learning as well as his self-esteem. This is all the more reason to identify your child's learning style and not put labels on him like "smart," "dumb," or "bad reader." It is also important for you to communicate with the teacher about your child's positive traits.

In order to avoid the self-fulfilling prophecy, maintain a pragmatic problem-solving approach to the situation.

For example, a good way to approach a teacher is to say, "I have an active, high-spirited child. John is easily distracted. Maybe he would do better if he sat at the front of the class. I'm always available to talk about him." Frame your child's characteristics in a *positive* way. Focus on problem solving as a team rather than your child's personality or problems.

If your child feels your constant disapproval, your self-fulfilling prophecy will certainly come true.

HOW TO HELP YOUR CHILD LEARN

Look at school as one part of learning. If your child seems bored or unstimulated and is having troubles, offer the opportunity to talk to her about what she likes in the classroom, what subject areas excite her during the day, and what she doesn't like. Be curious about your child's anxieties and explore ways to give support and reduce these anxieties. Are there emotional issues underlying her boredom? Does she need more stimulation? Be your child's advocate and help her maximize her learning experiences.

The following approaches will help your child learn:

- Pick quiet places to study and read.
- Parents should provide creative outlets outside of school if the teacher does not provide them.
- Pick a specific time to do homework.
- Help your child to work independently, but help her get started.
- Tolerate your child's expression of frustration at learning new things. Empathize with her.
- Don't do homework for your child. Use encouraging language like, "I'm glad to answer your questions, but you'll have to do the work by yourself."
- Check in with your child periodically, a practice to which you both agree, so that homework can progress and frustration is minimized.
- Set reasonable parameters around homework. Discuss how much time is needed for each subject. Look at the work and decide together how best to complete the task.

- Help organize tasks around your child's learning skills. For example, when six-year-old Johnny was learning subtraction, he was having trouble grasping the concept. Since Johnny was a visual learner, his mother used apples, pickles, and cookies to help teach him subtraction. It was more effective than writing $4 - 2 = 2$.
- Try to understand how the teacher teaches basic subjects like math and reading so that you can explain to your child in the same learning style.

Communicate with your child and really listen to his answers. This is the key to helping him.

HOW TO HELP YOUR CHILD DEVELOP THE SKILL OF INDEPENDENT LEARNING

Most parents cherish the moment when they see their children working on homework or a project independently. How does this happen? It's not easy. Working independently requires intrinsic motivation, or an attitude in you and in your child that says: *"I love to learn!"* Intrinsic (or internal) motivation begins to happen when you appreciate and acknowledge the times you see your children working, studying, and learning on their own. You can say, "It's great to see you learning so many new things." This attitude communicates that you value their independent efforts.

I remember the story that Leo Buscaglia, the famous author and educator, told about his father at dinner. Each night at supper, Leo's father—with much gusto and ceremony—would ask each of his children, "Tell me one thing that you learned at school today!'' With each child's answer he would beam. Leo's father did not ask about grades or scores on tests; he was only interested in learning. Each child had to think about what he or she had learned and share it with the family. This seems like a perfect example of how to encourage your children not only to value learning, but also to succeed independently.

Ultimately, children need to take ownership and responsibility for their learning and their work. We cannot impose our desire for them to learn. Otherwise, we create tension, resistance, and disappointment. We can only encourage and support them by our actions and our words.

Let's take the situation where you want your child to appreciate reading on his own and focus on the following actions:

- **Exposure**—Buy lots of books, go to the library.
- **Modeling**—Read a lot. Read the newspaper, discuss books.
- **Vicarious learning**—A child will observe how you learn and solve problems and will emulate you.

HOW TO GET A CHILD REFOCUSED ON A TASK

Challengers get easily distracted and are typically disorganized. You might view this as a discipline problem, but it's not. Rather, it's an issue of how your child organizes his world.

A challenging child is usually highly distractible. One mom yelled and nagged her daughter to do her homework, but the child couldn't get started. She would play with her art materials, look at the pictures in her reading book, and play with her pencils. The mother became increasingly irritated. She wanted to criticize her daughter for being so lazy, but the girl wasn't being oppositional. She was having trouble concentrating on her work and didn't have the actual skills to get started.

BREAK DOWN THE TASKS

You can help your child study by breaking down the tasks.

- Help your child structure his time by dividing tasks into small, manageable parts.
- Ask, "Does looking at the pictures in the story help you remember it better? How? What other ways will help you study?"
- Make sure your child has had an opportunity to release some energy before sitting down to study.
- Sometimes, building in breaks every 20 to 30 minutes (depending on age and length of break) is helpful.
- Offer your help in the beginning. Auditory learners, for example, need to hear the material read aloud.

CHILD ISSUES

Homework

Every parent would like their child to love school. But this isn't always the case with a challenger who has difficulty sitting and focusing on school work all day and then doing more work when he comes home.

Susan Levine advocates that children play first before doing homework. Of course, any parent of a challenging child is afraid to open those flood gates for fear the child will get so wild she will never get him settled down.

Ms. Levine feels that because challengers have to sit all day in school, after school they need to be physically active— to let loose a bit before they are required to sit down again and concentrate. Otherwise, a child may feel resistant and resentful of doing homework.

"Play is important," stresses Ms. Levine. "It's where challengers do most of their learning and creating." The child should feel he is winning at something. Give him some freedom after school, but set strict guidelines about when homework *does* begin.

Report Cards

Parents have traditionally placed an enormous importance on the particular grade a child gets on his report card. Challenging children may have undetected learning disabilities that impact them academically. Parents compound the problem when they demand better grades. (See Chapter 7.)

You need to ask yourself, "What does my child's grade mean to me? Why is it so important? Why does 'average' upset me so much?"

Sometimes grades are a reflection of wishful thinking on your part. You project what you think your child should be doing. Of course, every parent wants his child to get A's. But for a very challenging child, where learning disabilities are more prevalent, high grades should not be the overriding goal. Instead, help your youngster focus on the love of learning.

LOVING TO LEARN THROUGH MOTIVATION

It is important to motivate children, especially challengers who tend to be competitive.

If you have a gut feeling that your challenger is not working up to his potential, and you feel he can do better, share your concerns with your child. But the main objective in school should be for him to gain a love of learning, which is achieved by focusing on his efforts, not the results. If a child is excited about going to school, then he will be motivated to learn, and good grades will be a by-product.

The best way to assist your child is to help him become self-motivated. It is more important that he enjoy reading, not that he is the best reader in the class or that he receive a reward for reading. Your child needs to discover the pleasure himself. If your challenger likes to write stories, great! Don't focus on the spelling mistakes. The act of creating and being stimulated by new information should be the goal of parents and teachers alike. The art of fine-tuning spelling and handwriting will come in time. A motivated child will do well. As for the other tasks, work with your child at home in a relaxed and fun way.

The overuse of rewards can interfere with a child's love of learning. He may only focus on the reward. A child who gets $1.00 for every A in math will lose the desire to learn if the dollars stop the first time he gets a B.

Rewards can be given, but should be done in a thoughtful manner. A reward should not be seen as a bribe. Reward your child's *efforts*. If he gets a C but has studied hard and tried to do well, then reward his maximum effort, not the particular grade. This will further enhance his love of learning.

Together, look for ways to problem solve. Make sure your child is getting what he needs in school and be an advocate for his success.

Parent Plan

Use the following plan to help motivate your child:

- It's important to acknowledge your child's feelings when he says he doesn't like something. Let him know you appreciate his efforts and that you understand that he doesn't like math, but everyone has to learn it.
- Often parents have unrealistic ideas about what their child should be accomplishing. Many internal factors can affect a challenger's performance. Therefore, offering money for straight A's, can frustrate a challenger who feels this will never happen. He may just give up.
- Let your child do her schoolwork in her own way. Avoid criticizing, hovering, or giving constant directions. Otherwise she will feel that no matter what she does, it isn't good enough.
- Praise your child's efforts. By doing so you will motivate her to do the most important task—to try.

All of these motivational techniques will help teach self-discipline which is a useful behavioral tool for a challenger.

PARENT ADMINISTRATIVE ISSUES

It is important to communicate with the administrators of your child's school to let them know what your child's special needs are, and to find out how they can be a help and support. Once administrators understand that your child may have learning and behavior disabilities, they can work with the teachers to allay behavior problems, assist with medication needs, and facilitate educational testing.

Administrators can also be the key link in assisting you to pick the best teacher for your child. Don't worry about feeling like a "pushy" parent. Your child needs your help. You don't want him to be singled out, so approach the principal, counselor, or headmaster early on with any of your concerns.

CHILD RIGHTS

There is help for children. The laws, although different from state to state, usually insure that children are protected and guarantee the right to an appropriate education. There are reading specialists, language specialists, ESL teachers, and psychologists who can intervene when a child is having a learning or behavior problem.

Ask your child's school administrator or teacher what is the procedure for testing children. Most school systems are required to fund programs for children with learning disabilities or, conversely, offer enriched classes for gifted children.

What becomes important is early diagnosis so that your child can be in a program that is appropriate for him; otherwise he could be overlooked for years and then struggle in the upper grades or feel bored and understimulated.

Of course, you should try to provide enrichment activities as well for your child. Rather than overwhelm him, focus on the activities he excels in and seek help in areas where he is weak.

School can become a wonderful, exciting time for your child *if* you take the steps necessary to insure he will have a successful and enriched experience.

6

Social Challenges

How a challenging child relates to others socially is the basis for his character and how well he will fare in the world. Positive interaction can help a challenger feel good about himself. But parents must inevitably guide their child, giving him the appropriate social skills that will lead him into successful relationships in school, at home, and with friends. As we discussed in Chapter 2, children with good interpersonal skills are able to interact well with their friends.

Some of these positive social traits include:

- Cooperation
- Sharing
- Listening
- Understanding others' feelings (empathy)
- Tact
- Flexibility
- Sensitivity

The challenger who struggles with some or all of these traits needs to be taught these skills in order to recognize when he has hurt someone's feelings. Ignoring inappropriate social behavior or getting angry does not teach the skills your challenger needs in order to succeed. He will only feel confused, afraid, and alone and may develop low self-esteem, as a result.

The very nature of a challenger may put him in ready position for conflict. The challenging child often can't help himself, because he misreads social cues. A challenger might do something socially inappropriate and have no idea what he did wrong. When others reject him, he feels confused and withdraws.

A parent may want to compensate for his child's social difficulties by pushing him into activities like sports camp, gymnastics, or dance classes, hoping that these opportunities for interaction will draw him out and cure the social awkwardness. The problem is not about the child's inactivity, but rather his anxiety and confusion when placed in these social situations. The parent needs to recognize and address his challenger's anxiety first, then help him with the skills needed to cope with each situation.

HOW TO HELP YOUR CHILD IN SOCIAL SITUATIONS

- Reassure your child. Let him know that you are on his side.
- Help your child become more aware of his actions. Ask, "Did you notice your voice was getting loud?"

- Don't push your child into social situations where you know he will be uncomfortable and anxious.
- Don't embarrass your child if he makes a social "mistake."
- Draw your child's attention to the moments when he hurts your feelings or acts inappropriately.

PEER CHALLENGE

School is one of the most important areas of social learning for children. The classroom, the hall, the playground, before and after school, waiting in line for the bus, and walking home are all life-settings for social interactions. In these environments, children encounter younger and older kids. They learn to respond to a constantly changing and ultimately challenging environment. Even the easiest-going kids are often frazzled by one experience or another during a school day. For challenging children, the social context of school may be overwhelming. They must learn the cues other children give that indicate who's being included or excluded in order to navigate through the mine field of an average school day.

Let's take an everyday example. Suppose your challenger wants to play handball with some kids. Unaware of his own behavior, the challenger might jump in, appear loud and bossy and aggressive. A child who is able to read social context will hang around, watch, talk quietly, say, "That was a good shot," and will wait to be invited in or ask if he can play. He'll be available, but not pushy. He will have an understanding of the steps it takes to build friendships.

For elementary school children, friendships tend to come

and go. One day they have a best friend, the next day that friend is their enemy. A challenging child struggles to learn and read the normal teasing, taunts, and interactions of others. These incidents can be a source of anxiety for the challenger because each situation may become amplified into a crisis.

A challenger may feel overwhelmed and upset in the everyday interactions on the playground where teasing and name-calling is a regular occurrence. He may take the teasing personally, and react volatilely because he doesn't have the understanding that enables him not to take these normal childhood occurrences personally. Where you or I may be less likely to overreact, for a challenger, it is much more difficult to ignore or laugh off others' behavior. He gets hooked in, and then because he reacts emotionally with tears or anger, is labeled too sensitive. He becomes anxious and responds by further overreacting and escalating.

A challenger is highly sensitive to his friends' approval or disapproval, but because of his difficulty containing his feelings, may react inappropriately. In this way, the challenger can leave himself open for criticism and rejection.

Ironically, a challenger wants friends more than anything. But children can sometimes reject a challenging child because of his very nature. Although the big guns are usually reserved for parents, friends often get a dose of difficult behavior as is shown in the case of eight-year-old Jason.

Jason was a high-strung child. He was competitive, strong-willed, and volatile. At school, kids were more willing to accept his behavior. But when Jason was invited over to a classmate's house for a birthday party, there was nothing but trouble.

Jason wanted to run all around the house. He pulled out games and toys and left them sitting scattered in his friend's room. When Kenny asked him to clean up, Jason felt singled out. He started to whine, protest, and escalate until Kenny's mother asked him to calm down or she would have to take him home.

Jason pushed in line to be the first one to hit the piñata and eat the birthday cake. His classmates were getting angry, which was only exacerbated by the reaction and disapproval from other parents. Jason's friends withdrew from him and complained about his behavior. One boy even told him, "You're too wild, and every time I play with you I get in trouble."

Jason became more and more withdrawn as his friends shunned him. As a result, he felt hurt and angry, which only made him act out more.

Jason needed a plan to help him discuss his feelings and understand his behavior before spending time with his friends. Challengers need very specific guidance with social boundaries. Parents need to let their child know when they've gone too far with a friend and what is acceptable or unacceptable.

You can teach social skills in a loving and nonjudgmental way. The challenging child, may experience his day as going from one crisis to another without a respite. Here's how to help your challenging child turn the day around.

Parent Plan

- Set time limits on play dates. Two hours is usually sufficient for an afterschool play date. Be consistent, and do not give in if your child tries to push the limit you've established. Say, "If today works out, then next time I will consider extending the time."

- Have just a few friends over at a time. Actually, one is ideal.
- Set clear behavior expectations. Say, "If you are not able to cooperate, I will use a time-out."
- In new or unfamiliar situations, ask your child, "How would you like your friends to treat you?" You should give feedback to your child to bring him to a state of awareness. For instance, "Jason, I saw you shove Andy when he wouldn't play with you. Were you aware of your behavior? How could you have expressed in words your frustration to Andy?"
- Have your child role-play with stuffed animals or puppets. Play out a negative situation in order to explore what your child is feeling. Because a challenging child often reacts impulsively and doesn't think about his feelings, he may be unaware of his actions in a social situation. Role-playing helps your child separate himself from the situation.
- Drawing pictures is a good technique to help a challenger focus his attention and express his feelings. Once the drawing is complete, you can ask open-ended questions like, "If the picture could talk, what would it be saying?"
- Do not expect instant success. Allow for mistakes and keep working at it.

A challenger needs to learn to express his feelings, what he likes and dislikes—especially about friends—no matter what technique you use.

TRANSITION CHALLENGES

Part of the problem a challenger has in social situations emanates from his inability to make a transition. Challengers get turned on like a motor but don't know how to turn off.

A situation might occur where you are tickling or rough-housing with your child, and you say, "Okay, that's enough," but he still wants to play. Again, you let him know that the play is over, but he is wild and unwilling to stop.

You become bothered. "Okay, I said, enough!" But your child *can't stop*. By now, things are out of control. The fun you were having together has turned into an angry confrontation; you are upset and exhausted and your child is unhappy.

Challengers have difficulty with change, starting new projects, and transitions from one activity or place to another. There is a great amount of anxiety over these transitional moments.

Because any change is frightening and disorienting, a challenger will use control in order to reduce his anxiety. In social situations, he may appear stubborn and disobedient. Often the transition of leaving a friend's house can become a big issue. Disconnecting is difficult.

For four-year-old Julie transitions created an enormous amount of anxiety. She got upset when her little friend left after a play date. She cried, ran after her, and literally flailed on the ground. Her mother was anxious about arranging play dates in the future because Julie's behavior was out-of-hand, and there was no clear way to help her.

A challenger is like a top. He gets all wound up tightly, and when he starts to unwind, he is all over the place. It's hard to stop him, and if you do, he unravels and falls apart.

Transitions often leave a parent disappointed, frustrated, and exhausted, and she attributes the problem to her child being unmanageable or not listening. The truth is that during transitions your child is so anxious that he is unable to hear you, and your challenge is to help him through it.

A parent often gets angry at her child when he "loses it" during transitions and that only exacerbates the problem. The entire family can play a big role in helping the challenger get through transitions. The key points are:

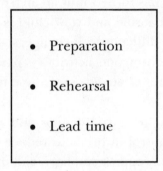

- Preparation

- Rehearsal

- Lead time

- **Prepare kids in advance** Before an event, have a family meeting to explain what you expect to happen. Will there be long lines, a wait, loud noises, etc.? When kids are included in the process, they take some ownership. Talk about your expectations of your child's behavior.
- **Rehearse** Include your child in the discussion about transitions. Ask, "How can we help you through this time?" It becomes cooperative problem solving when

you engage your child in an open dialogue. Talk about his fears. It's important for him to feel included. This creates intimacy and closeness and eases anxiety. Role-play the situation.

- **Lead time** Tell friends or relatives that your child sometimes has difficulty with transitions, and that he may have a hard time when it's time to leave. Set it up in advance. This helps diffuse the situation at the onset, and eases the parent's anticipatory anxiety about his child's behavior.

Challengers in the midst of a transitional tantrum may project their behavior onto their parent. For instance, when Brent's mom was trying to calmly talk to him during his tantrum (he was crying and yelling), he said, "Why are you yelling at me?" Ellen was perplexed. She wasn't yelling, he was.

At this point, Ellen's options are: 1) leave the room; 2) engage in a conversation about how she wasn't yelling; or 3) remain silent and let her son de-escalate.

Let's discuss each: 1) If Ellen leaves the room, she should say, "When you finish crying, meet me in the den and we can talk about it." 2) Engaging in a conversation will only increase the crying because Brent is getting attention for his behavior. This is not such a good idea. 3) Sitting quietly is effective if Ellen can be supportive and comforting without trying to get her son to stop crying. She can say, "I know you're upset. It's okay. I'll sit next to you. When you finish crying, we can talk." Then, she should remain silent without getting upset.

HOW DO CHALLENGERS PERCEIVE TRANSITIONS?

A challenger faced with a new situation does not have the internal mechanism to "filter" his emotional experiences. Change is disturbing and threatening; therefore the challenger is resistant to new situations. His anxiety causes him to appear oppositional or defiant when he is actually afraid. He overreacts or escalates because of an inability to contain his anxieties.

Sometimes a challenger struggles internally with these fears although externally he doesn't seem frightened. In fact, sometimes he appears extroverted and overly confident. In truth, he is overcompensating for his anxiety. For instance, in a group situation, he will try to control or dominate the group because he doesn't know how to contain his anxiety. His emotions intrude on his interactions.

For the parent, the challenge is not to criticize or get into a power struggle with your child. Once you understand his apparent defiance as anxiety or fear, you will be able to strategize and problem solve. Let's look at the following everyday school experience that can turn into a nightmare:

Situation
Challenger is asked to read aloud

↓

Internal Feeling
Anxiety, fear, feeling out of control—afraid to make a
mistake and be humiliated in front of his friends

↓

External Action

Makes up words, giggles, whispers, disturbs the class

↓

Prescription

Help your child translate his external actions into feelings that can be addressed. For example you might say, "I guess you are nervous about reading this new book. I'll be happy to help you with the hard words. It's a great story." Another strategy might be to say, "Does it help you to know that all kids have fears about reading? Would you like to go first or go last? Would you rather begin reading privately or out loud."

The goal is to strategize ways to increase your child's comfort and feeling of being in control by reducing his fear.

SOCIAL INTERACTIONS

Challenging children are subject to intense reactions from other parents. Your child's struggles can bring your own past hurts into focus, and rekindle painful feelings from your own childhood.

Jenny was a popular but challenging seven-year-old. She was high-spirited and active. When her friends decided to get together for a weekly swim club at each others' houses, Jenny was elated. She ran home to tell her mom.

That night, Carol received a call from one of the mothers of the girls who had planned the swim club. The mother told her that Jenny was being excluded from the club because they already had four girls and a fifth would not be a good idea. But these were Jenny's best friends.

Carol immediately suspected that there was another reason for Jenny's exclusion. Carol had heard from her friends that these mothers thought that Jenny was too wild and too difficult to handle.

Carol felt hurt by the other mothers criticizing her child. In truth, she felt as if she was being rejected. She realized that she was overreacting, and Jenny needed help. Carol had to face the fact that this was Jenny's problem and not hers.

Carol used the following parent plan to help Jenny and herself get through this sensitive issue.

Parent Plan

- You must explore and acknowledge your own feelings as you help your child explore hers.
- Ask your child what she thinks people mean when they call her "difficult."
- Say to your child, "Are you aware when you cross the line?"
- A parent cannot "change" a child's feelings. She feels what she feels, and you cannot change that, but you can help her understand.
- How do you handle other parents? Do not yell or try to defend your child. Explain that your child's feelings were hurt, and say, "Can we work this out before it gets out of control? I would be glad to plan a strategy that has worked with other friends."

- Children need time apart from each other and parents. One solution might be to plan for quiet time during the day.

CO-OP PARENTING

Cooperative parenting means soliciting the cooperation of other parents to help your challenger in difficult situations. This is especially useful if you are a single parent or when you are at work or otherwise unavailable.

Cooperative parenting avoids blame, finger-pointing, and criticism and helps create a positive atmosphere for change. Cooperative parenting is a way to share ideas and thoughts with parents in a non-accusatory or non-threatening way. Enlist cooperative parenting in understanding each other's children by offering to do tasks, asking questions, and sharing stories and personal experiences.

Carol could, for example, make a plan with the other mothers and say, "I will let Jenny know in advance that the rules at our house apply at yours too. If she gets too rowdy . . .

- . . . ask her to relax. Make her aware of her behavior."
- . . . call me. I'll pick her up."
- . . . if you feel comfortable, give her a time-out."

- "In turn, if you have problems that you would like me to handle with your child when she comes over, I will. For instance, if you would like to know if she helps pick up toys at clean-up time, if she cooperates, if there are food restrictions that you would like carried through, let me know."

Support each other. Don't be afraid to ask questions. Don't place blame on each other's children or each other. This is the first and most important step toward cooperative parenting.

THE HELPLINE LIFELINE

Support is vital for parents of a challenging child. It is often difficult to talk about your child even to good friends and especially relatives because they may not understand your struggles unless they too have raised a challenging child. There is a special bond between people with like experiences. You can obtain support group information through your religious affiliation, your child's school, the local mental health center, hospitals, and pediatricians' offices. If you can't find a group specifically for challenging children, then start one. Share stories, books, new theories, articles, discipline techniques, and information about your own lives. Share the good and wonderful things about your children. Try to find a positive perspective, and if possible, see the humor in your struggles together.

Challenging children often bring us to tears because we feel so alone. The challenge lies in our understanding and our willingness to expose our mistakes to others, so we can learn together how to be a more effective parent.

PHYSICALLY ACTIVE CHALLENGERS

If you are going to help your challenger socially, then you need to find activities that help him feel good about himself. A challenger may be, by nature, active, so one of the best ways to help him release some of his energy is through sports. Challengers may have difficulty with social interactions, so team sports may help your child learn how to interact socially.

At first you might want to suggest sports like gymnastics, tennis, dance, or swimming where your child can learn to derive satisfaction from his own efforts and obtain a sense of individual accomplishment.

If you do choose a team sport, then you may need to help your challenger with concepts like fair play, good sportsmanship, how a team wins or loses *as a unit,* joining in, and the child's value as a part of the team.

Some challengers are so competitive that if they do not immediately excel at a sport, they will show disinterest and even give up.

A parent can get overinvolved in his child's sports activities, and this can be detrimental. As we mentioned in Chapter 4, parental internal responses are often likened to their own personal experiences as children. How many times have you seen a father yelling at his child for striking out or missing a ball? Our wish for our child is to win, not just in sports, but in life. This push to win can be harmful to a challenger who is sensitive, already competitive, and highly charged.

Sports can be helpful in learning discipline, perseverance, concentration, tolerance, and how to develop friendships. Succeeding at a sport is not always measured by winning. You can push a challenging child too far by making demands on him to be a good athlete. The original intention can get lost.

You can transfer the pressure *you* felt as a child to your own child. Subconsciously you think that his winning means you're winning. The irony is, even if he wins the game, he loses the value of sports, which is to make friends, reduce stress, and have fun.

Parent Plan

- Choose a sport which is appropriate for your child's personality, not one that you like.
- Do not overpraise or criticize your child's effort. Say, "Good game," and leave it at that. Let your child do some self-assessment.
- Practice containing your own feelings regarding competition and the need to win. Let the experience be your child's.
- Never compare your child to other players.

THE VALUE OF COMPETITIVE PLAY

Children need to play—especially challengers. Play becomes a creative as well as physical outlet for challenging kids and provides an opportunity for you to participate with your child—to get close and create both physical and emotional contact. But play can often escalate into disruptive social interactions because it invokes a sense of competition based on certain preset goals: who'll hit the most balls, get the highest score, run the fastest, and build the highest tower of blocks.

Competitive play doesn't have to become negative or cut-throat. It can be a rewarding, fun, and stimulating experience if approached correctly. Sports can help your child learn discipline, perseverance, and how to develop friendships. It is a healthy outlet for challengers.

Because challengers are by nature competitive, the desire to win at all costs is something parents should try to avoid. A challenger needs guidance in her play, and you can be the guide for your child.

Some of the more valuable lessons children can learn from competitive play are:

- Winning isn't everything.
- Persistence and hard work pay off.
- One can depend on teammates to help accomplish a goal.
- Competitive play is built into our society. While it can be exciting for a challenger, it can also separate her from others. Challengers, by nature, often see winning as a "need."
- The key is to focus on your child's effort, not on whether her team won.
- Support your youngster's incremental improvements in skills.

During competition we tend to focus on the result rather than the effort.

The competitive spirit needs to be used wisely. It is best not to use critical statements such as:

- "What's wrong with you?"
- "You're not working hard enough!"
- "Everyone else is doing better than you."

These statements undermine self-esteem and create distance between you and your child. There is a more supportive approach to competitive play—the idea that whether or not a child wins or loses, you are proud of his effort.

Give praise by using statements like:

- "I think it's great that you tried your best."
- "You really used good teamwork."
- "You were very involved."
- "Can I help you practice?"
- "It looked like you had a lot of fun!"
- "You're kicking the ball really far these days."

THE VALUE OF NON-COMPETITIVE PLAY

Non-competitive play emphasizes your child's efforts, not necessarily the result. Non-competitive play focuses on cooperative teamwork and fun. There is no emphasis on winners or losers.

The lessons in non-competitive play for challengers and parents are:

- You learn how your child perceives his world by how he interacts and approaches the game.
- Non-competitive play enhances intimacy and helps a

challenger in his social situations by showing others he is willing to play cooperatively without focusing on the outcome.

* Non-competitive play helps challengers have fun in a non-stressful atmosphere.

Activities

Look for activities that encourage interaction and curiosity, and for play that promotes closeness like:

* **Storytelling** Get your child involved in the story and books by asking questions. Encourage imaginative interaction by asking kids to make up their own stories.
* **Roughhousing** This promotes physical and emotional contact; activities like tumbling and tickling are fun and a great outlet for your challenger.
* **Art projects** Clay, paints, and crayons provide outlets for creativity and imagination, and let you learn about your child. Ask questions about the drawings and creations. Clay is a good outlet for tension.
* **Bike rides, skating, water play**
* **Computers**
* **Collecting** This is a good opportunity to include your child in something you love and get her started in an interesting project.
* **Building models**
* **Imaginative play** like "house," "school," "Power Rangers."

Remember that play, whether it be competitive or non-competitive, is an opportunity for your child to have fun, learn some valuable lessons about teamwork, and create a closer bond with you and friends.

THE SOCIALLY SHY CHALLENGER

Challengers who typically misread social cues may start to retreat socially because of the lack of positive reinforcement from schoolmates or friends. This is different from the child whose temperament it is to be shy inherently. Challengers rarely begin life as "shy" children. They tend to be active and expressive.

By labeling your child "shy," you avoid the fact that she may be having difficulties socially. You may be confusing his withdrawing because of anxiety with shyness. Moreover, once you label your child as "shy," you immediately categorize and stigmatize her. Shy children are often pushed aside by the phrase, "Oh, she's just shy," and left in social Siberia as if there is nothing that can be done about it. But there are strategies you can use to help your child.

Parent Plan

- Avoid labels like "shy," "withdrawn," "timid."
- Make changes step-by-step and go slowly. Don't force your child into uncomfortable situations. The technique of "throwing your child in the pool so he can

learn to swim" is not the answer to helping a shy child in social situations.

- Let your child choose the place or event you are going to attend.
- Prepare your child in advance, and give her some idea of what to expect.
- Involve your child in activities that are interesting or fun, where she may meet other children with similar interests whom she can befriend.

If you can help your challenging child create positive social interactions, you have given him the tools to start his adult life. Without give and take, sensitivity to others' feelings, and a sense of fairness, healthy social relationships cannot take place.

Your overall goal in social interactions is to enable your challenging child to articulate her feelings. The more you can help her do this, the better she will be able to express feelings to her friends and the better she'll feel about herself.

7

More Challenging Challengers

This chapter is meant as an introduction to the topic of Attention Deficit Disorder (ADD). Many excellent books deal exclusively with the problem of attention deficit including *Why Johnny Can't Concentrate: Coping with Attention Deficit Problems* by Robert A. Moss, M.D.

In this chapter, we will focus on the characteristics of ADD, the testing process, and the issue of medication. In the process, we will raise questions that many parents ask, and give answers so you can make decisions to effectively help your child.

Note: ADD refers to children with Attention Deficit Disorder. This means that your child may be highly distractible, unable to focus for long periods of time, and unable to retain information. ADHD refers to children who exhibit not only the above behaviors, but are also fidgety, constantly moving, and unable to ignore sensory stimulation such as noises, scents, and sights. According to Barbara D. Ingersol, Ph.D., and Sam Goldstein, Ph.D., children with learning disabilities experience a discrepancy of at least 20 points between intelligence test scores and achievement test scores. These discrepancies show up on tests of oral expression (speaking), listening comprehension (understanding), written expression, basic reading, reading comprehension, mathematics calculation, and mathematics reasoning (problem solving).

There can be overlap between challenging children, ADD children, and kids with learning disabilities. Often it is a matter of degree.

Challengers with ADD or ADHD can have other learning disabilities such as dyslexia. However, children with other learning disabilities do not necessarily have ADD or ADHD. For the purposes of this chapter, we will focus primarily on ADD.

How severely your child is distracted and how regularly he has problems necessitates further testing and determines which interventions will be most effective. It is vital to get a professional to test your child and then work with a psychologist or psychiatrist in order to determine if your challenger has an attention deficit problem.

You need to find out where the attention deficit exists. Even challengers who do not have as severe a problem as ADD may feel enormous anguish over their own difficulties with concentration.

The value of testing is to help define the areas of strength and difficulty for each child. As Dr. Moss points out in *Why Johnny Can't Concentrate,* many ADD children go undetected for years because they appear to be listening and not bothering others; therefore, a teacher might conclude that the child doesn't have a problem. But if your child is having difficulty focusing on his school subject matter, the problem may certainly lie with ADD.

There is a line between challenging children and children with ADD, but that line is not always clearly drawn. Proper testing will help delineate these distinctions. You may have some fear that if you have your child tested, the result is etched in stone. In truth, it is a source of relief for the child and the parent to find out what's wrong and to deal with it as a problem with a solution.

WHAT'S WRONG WITH MY CHILD?

You have a funny feeling in the pit of your stomach. Something is not right with your child. You pick up different books about children with ADD and hyperactive kids, difficult children, and gifted children, but you still haven't a clue. One minute your child is doing great, the next, she is struggling. You ask yourself, "What's wrong with my child?" But children can be a myriad of things—wonderful, challenging, ADD, gifted, and have learning disabilities all at the same time.

The parents of ADD children face enormous demands. Bobby struggled for 20 years without fully understanding why he was so unhappy. Bobby, now an adult, had profound emotional problems from the time he was a toddler. He had angry outbursts. He could not take any criticism or disruption in his life. He had tantrums when things didn't go his way even as a teenager. He felt victimized, frustrated, and frightened. His younger sister began having nightmares. She was afraid to be at home alone with him.

The family finally went for counseling when Bobby was 13 years old. While discussing family history, the therapist learned that Bobby often felt different, distracted, lazy, and stupid.

Bobby was tested one-on-one for learning disabilities at age eight and shown to have no learning disabilities and a fairly high I.Q. His social problems went undiagnosed as well. He wet his bed and was afraid to go to friends' homes. He was small and immature for his age and spent most of his time isolated from other kids.

Three years passed, and the problems continued. He was retested, but no learning disabilities surfaced. He became more and more isolated at school and began to feel "dumb." His self-esteem, already fragile, was painfully low. He did just enough work to get by. Nevertheless, under duress, he did apply himself and at times did well.

Over the years, his parents tried to encourage him. They offered every possible option to their son. In the end, nothing worked. He resisted new experiences because he was terrified to fail, frightened of rejection, and confused as to what to do.

He barely managed to graduate from high school. At this point, his therapist tried to convince him to get tested for ADD and other disabilities that he had never been tested for. He still resisted.

He went to junior college but couldn't keep up, which further damaged his self-esteem. After enough trust was built up with his therapist, he finally agreed to testing.

The results showed that his overwhelming emotional problems (critical thoughts/social isolation) were influencing his academic achievement. This helped him recognize that his emotional state was interfering with his progress.

His anxiety was so great that it confounded his test results. Again, the educational therapists were unable to identify the problem.

Bobby was finally stimulated by his love of art. His father

was a well-known painter, but Bobby was afraid to fail in comparison to his dad's accomplishments. He was a visual learner and started to dabble with different media, but had trouble sticking to it. Teachers encouraged him, but he had trouble concentrating and didn't know why. He became depressed.

The psychologist started to consider the possibility that Bobby had neurological problems and suggested Bobby meet with a psychiatrist for medication. Bobby was extremely resistant to this idea.

By the time he was 20 years old, however, Bobby acknowledged that he needed to deal with his depression. He began taking anti-depressant medication. He still wondered why he was so distracted and unable to concentrate. One evening, he saw a television program about ADD, and he recognized himself.

After another round of testing, ADD was finally diagnosed. His self-esteem increased, just knowing what was wrong, just knowing it wasn't him, that he wasn't stupid or lazy.

There were many other challenges with Bobby over the years that had been in the way of a proper diagnosis. From time to time Bobby would feel hopeless, believing that as much as he tried to make things better, nothing worked. At other times, memories of his past failures would enrage and immobilize him. Moreover, his friendships were few, and his fears of rejection left him isolated socially, and mostly a loner. Obviously, his parents were anguished thinking they didn't do enough for Bobby. Yet, no one caught it. A parent can intercede in all aspects of a child's life and think he has a clearer picture of what may be necessary to help him, and still not be able to change things.

A child with ADD and other emotional problems affects

all family interactions as well as other areas of the child's life. For this reason alone, you need to explore all aspects of testing and psychological counseling until your child is helped. Understanding and knowledge about your child can empower you.

WHAT LOOKS LIKE ADD TO A CHALLENGED PARENT

Perhaps your child is having emotional problems and acting out, and so you worry that your child has ADD. Maybe she has a neurological problem or a learning disability, and you may also confuse this with ADD. Although there is overlap in the emotional and neurological aspects of ADD, it is not always so clear-cut. When a parent suspects that his child might have ADD, then each piece of the equation has to be dealt with— genetic, psychological, biological.

Children with ADD sometimes have emotional problems which will need to be addressed. The child may appear depressed or anxious. This may indicate some chemical imbalances. If a proper assessment is not made, you could deal with your child's learning disability and miss the biochemical aspect. This is why early and proper diagnosis is important. Most psychologists suggest children get tested when they are about six years of age, or earlier.

Children with ADD don't know what's wrong with them. They tend to act out, get in trouble in school, perhaps get rejected by other children, and may need constant limits. Therefore, it is a source of relief for both the child and the parent to identify the problem and to deal with it in a thoughtful way. The reverse can also be true.

Leslie was surprised to find out her son did not have ADD. She thought that a diagnosis would help her understand her child. But Greg, a very challenging nine-year-old, needed more work, different discipline techniques, and more emotional counseling in order to help him get under control. Leslie also needed some counseling as well as better parenting skills so that she could be a successful parent to her son.

There are a myriad of learning disabilities that a challenging child may have that may *appear* to be ADD, but in fact are not. An excellently trained psychologist/tester can pick up the differences. In *Why Johnny Can't Concentrate,* it is pointed out that the traits most associated with ADD are:

- **Auditory and Language Problems** Difficulty with sounds of words and speech process problems which can lead to both inattention and concentration problems.
- **Fine Motor Difficulties** Trouble using pencils, crayons, and scissors, which leads to frustration for children.
- **Visual Perception Problems** Reversing letters and words, decoding backwards, reading problems.
- **Sequencing Difficulties** Inability to get things in correct order and follow multistep directions. This can be very frustrating for a child and can lead to lack of attention.
- **Poor Memory Skills** A child's ability to learn is impacted by poor memory and appears to be a focus problem.

This is where testing is beneficial. Even if your child has many of the above traits, a list of characteristics does not necessarily mean he does or does not have ADD.

THE ROLE OF TESTING FOR CHALLENGERS

Can testing be helpful to challenging kids? Most psychologists think so. A challenging child tends to perplex a parent or teacher who pins labels on him everytime the challenger's moods change—hyperactive, gifted, learning disabled. . . . Testing is a tool that provides a baseline understanding of the child and helps distinguish between ADD children and challengers. Testing can also bring out the good qualities your child possesses so he can reach his highest potential.

Think about the first time you read a book about diseases. Chances are you thought you had symptoms of every disease you read about. We often evaluate our children the same way. But a challenging child needs a more careful assessment because he may or may not be anything more than "challenging." Testing can be a guide to help us help our children get the proper tools necessary to maximize learning and social interaction.

The key to testing is to be prepared with the proper questions, so that you are not intimidated by information that may seem foreign or uncomfortable. Once you have decided to get your child tested, work as a team with the therapist. Anne Panofsky-Eisenberg, Ph.D., a Los Angeles psychologist, suggests parents ask themselves the following questions:

1. How long has my child been acting this way? Since birth? At three?
2. How pervasive is this behavior? Three hours a day, all day, only in a loud environment?
3. What can we do at home to change things? Research

has indicated that what goes on at home can match what goes on in school.

4. Should my child be in a different school environment?
5. Is there a learning disorder?
6. Are there neurological problems? Psychological problems?

When these questions have been explored, the therapist should take a detailed family history to see if there is ADD in the genetic family link.

One high-achieving, fast-track couple couldn't understand how they had such an intensely active child. But with some exploration of their own childhood and adult behaviors, the parents realized that their child was very much a reflection of themselves—hyper, strong-willed, dynamic, and verbal.

Of course this is not always the case, as Dr. Marion Schulman, a Los Angeles neuropsychologist, points out. ADD can be acquired later in life by head injuries or even whiplash. That's why psychological testing (feelings, social skills, and achievement) as well as neuropsychological testing (thought process, concentration, and learning) is necessary to detect ADD.

Another key to why testing is important is that, as Dr. Schulman points out, "An ADD child may be depressed and need help, but it's hard to diagnose the depression because of his hyper behavior. Instead, the child's personality is reflected in low self-esteem, sadness in his drawings, and angry behavior."

In order to begin the process of helping your child, you need a basic understanding of some terms that are used in the field of testing.

Baseline is a starting point. It allows you to properly assess your child's needs in order to begin the correct intervention. Baseline gives kids and parents a reference point so they can see the changes that take place over time.

Dr. Panofsky-Eisenberg has tested hundreds of children over the years. She quotes psychologist Larry Silver's definition of ADD which he equates with the workings of a car:

Hyperactive The brakes aren't working.
Distractibility/Short Attention Span The filter isn't working.
Impulsive The circuits are misfiring.

Let's look at the traits of ADD more closely as further outlined by Dr. Robert Moss in *Why Johnny Can't Concentrate:*

Hyperactivity

A hyperactive child is constantly and excessively moving his body, fidgeting, and has trouble sitting quietly for any length of time.

Distractibility

Often a child with ADD is fine on a one-to-one basis, but in a classroom, it may be impossible for her to focus on the activities in the room. She will listen to the teacher, but can lose her entire focus just by someone coughing or a pencil tapping. An ADD child also has trouble completing her schoolwork. Her mind wanders, and she tends to think about all sorts of things except her work.

Impulsivity

An impulsive child tends to make a lot of errors in her schoolwork because she may rush to get everything completed. For instance, she may add instead of subtract because she does not take the time to see if the sign has changed. One little girl always left out "a," "and," and "the" from her sentences because she wanted to finish quickly.

Disorganization

An ADD child will forget appointments, leave jackets and notebooks at school, and forget to turn in her work. A sense of structure seems to be missing even if her parents go to great lengths to organize her life. Her room may be messy, Some kids are also disorganized about their appearance.

Although there are books written about the definitions of ADD, the above traits are primary and almost constant with ADD children. These traits may overlap; many sound just like those of challengers. So don't start saying, "Oh yes, that's my child," because there are different degrees of ADD. (That's why there is so much misdiagnosis.) And we must stress again that assessing a child properly is what matters most.

THE TESTING PROCESS

It is better to test children before they enter school, so that emotional and self-esteem issues don't interfere with learning. During testing, psychologists look at numerous variables from a child's life.

- Environment (pollution such as lead, high power lines, medication taken during pregnancy)
- Inherited traits and parents' backgrounds
- Parents' relationship and the tenor of home life
- Abstract reasoning
- Vocabulary
- Visual-spatial relations
- Recognition of details
- Auditory processing (expressing and receiving information properly)

The main test that is given is an I.Q. test to establish a baseline. The rule of thumb is that ADD does not affect a child's intelligence but may impact on an I.Q. test score.

It usually takes up to eight hours or more over a period of days or weeks to complete a battery of tests. The educational therapist should try to get to know the child and help him feel comfortable, so that he will do his best.

I.Q. TESTS

In her book, *The Joys and Challenges of Raising a Gifted Child,* Susan Golant reminds us that "I.Q. tests measure only one aspect of intelligence—analytic reasoning—but do little to assess the learning process, creativity, insight or other factors thought to be a part of intelligence."

I.Q. (Intelligence Quotient) measures the ratio between a child's mental age and his chronological age. If your seven-year-old scores like average seven-year-olds, his I.Q. would be around 100. The middle (normal) range—90% of the population—falls between 70-130. If your seven-year-old child scores like a 10-year-old, his score would be in the higher range— closer to 130.

The following scale gives a basic guideline for evaluating I.Q.:

70–80 *Borderline between normal and retarded*
90–110 *Average range* Your child would be able to perform like a child his age. You can have an average I.Q. and still not perform like children your own age. Sometimes I.Q. and achievement tests don't match up.
110–120 *High average*
120–130 *Superior*
130–above *Very superior*

I.Q. scores are fixed. Many times a parent doesn't want to know his child's I.Q., fearing if it is low he will somehow have little expectation of his child, and the child will feel his disappointment. Or, if the score is high, the parent may place unrealistic expectations on his child, and show disappointment if he doesn't meet those goals. Because there are variations over the years, you need to understand what an I.Q. score means.

Dr. Schulman believes that I.Q. testing can pick up ADD. For instance, the mental arithmetic subtest gives timed problems. A child has to be able to do problems in his head. Because ADD kids have so much trouble concentrating and focusing, they often cannot do this test, certainly not in the time allotted.

I.Q. scores should in no way limit a child's ability to do well. The test gives information on the person's capacity and how he is functioning in the present—not in the future.

Dr. Panofsky-Eisenberg breaks down the testing into different parts.

I. THE WECHSLER INTELLIGENCE SCALE FOR CHILDREN (with 10 subtests) Some of the subtests measure:

- **Processing** This tests how quickly a child gives answers. A subtest would show how a child could match up designs on two sides of a page. This is called a symbol search.
- **Freedom from distractibility** Arithmetic skills would be a subtest in this category.
- **Verbal comprehension** One of the subtests evaluates the child's vocabulary.
- **Perceptual organization** A child puts blocks together on a picture. It also tests how a child puts mazes and puzzle parts together.

II. ACTERS This test gives a rating scale which looks for:

- **Hyperactivity** Can a child sit for any length of time? Is he fidgety? Does he keep his hands busy, act, or talk without thinking? Is he restless?
- **Oppositionality** Does the child start fights easily? Does he defy authority?
- **Attention span** Does the child follow a sequence of instructions and succeed with a task in a reasonable amount of time?
- **Social skills** How skilled is the child at making new friends? Does he follow social norms?

III. BENDER GESTALT This is the visual motor test which checks for neurological problems. For instance, the child copies designs. You ask him to draw what he sees. The child may draw dots. But instead of stopping, he will draw across and up the page because he can't stop. The child has trouble finding a boundary. This is called "perseveration."

IV. PROJECTIVES (Rorschach Inkblot Test) This tests how a child does without structure. If his inner process is organized, the test will reflect that. A person with ADD might be too quick to respond to the pictures shown. Some pictures look like people, some like bats or flowers. An impulsive person will see the picture and will respond quickly without noticing any of the overall details. He will see the whole and not any of the separate parts.

V. CREATIVITY TESTING This looks at divergent thinking (kids who travel to the beat of their own drums). Questions might include, "What would happen if fish no longer existed? If trees no longer existed? What would we do?"

Once a child has been tested, it is important to sit down with the educational psychologist and evaluate all aspects of the results. It's like putting a puzzle together. The results, along with the evaluation of your child, will enable you to make decisions about appropriate schools, medication, environment, discipline, and many other factors.

One 10-year-old girl, Sara, told her mom she had a dream. In the dream she wished that she would do better in school. She said she didn't understand why she couldn't do better and listen to the teacher. She was constantly frustrated.

When Sara was tested, she did not test ADD, but the tests gave her mother a clear picture of a perceptual learning disability. Judy was then able to get Sara the help she needed. In essence, her dream came true.

THE MEDICATION PUZZLE

There are many alternatives to medication depending on the severity of your child's attention deficit problem. Besides various behavioral and motivational techniques, Dr. Robert Moss, author of *Why Johnny Can't Concentrate* points out that some parents have actually found that giving their child a cup of caffeinated coffee has been beneficial because of the effect it has on the neurotransmitters in the brain (chemical substances that dispatch messages in the brain). But most doctors would agree that this is not the desired long-term treatment for a child with attention deficit problems.

If your child does have ADD, then your family can take steps to help him reach his highest potential. Dr. Marion Schulman suggests that you need to form a relationship with the child's school and teacher in an effort to maximize helping plan an effective medication treatment program.

Most important, a protocol involving medication should be undertaken only with the consultation of physicians, including a pediatrician and a psychiatrist. With your and your child's help, the physicians will be able to regulate the appropriate dosages, based on your child's response. Just because your neighbor's son does well on one dosage, does not mean that the same dosage is appropriate for your daughter. There are significant individual differences. In fact, for your child, medication may not be appropriate at all.

Since ADD is not something children just grow out of, the problems exacerbate as the child gets older. If not caught early, ADD can lead to serious emotional disruption. With the use of proper medication, some attention deficit problems have been proven to diminish 70% to 80%.

Dr. Panofsky-Eisenberg feels that if the proper medication can make your child more focused and help him concentrate and ultimately feel better about himself, then it is certainly worth the exploration.

Dr. Schulman feels that medication is an answer *only* after all other alternatives have been tried. The point of medication is to help a child focus in school and get better control of himself. A challenger, because he has all of the challenging traits, is not necessarily a candidate for medication. As we've explained, there are ways to help him behaviorally and psychologically. Challengers are difficult by nature, but their problems, unlike ADD children, may not be psychophysiological.

A quiet, introverted parent might think that his challenger has ADD, but in reality, this may not be the case. The perception of the child is altered by the parent/child match. (For more information on match, see Chapter 2, Conflict in Parent/Child Learning Styles.) These variables alone are reason to get a child tested early.

MEDICATIONS

Following are the medications most widely prescribed for children with ADD and ADHD. But there are new medications that doctors are trying and finding effective. Look into all possible avenues. Most parents are perplexed by the idea of giving a stimulant to a child who is already hyperactive. But it has been found that a stimulant works on the neurotransmitters in the brain and releases reserve ones, which actually increases the ability to focus. Dr. Moss advocates considering the following medications:

Stimulants:

Ritalin

The most well-known drug prescribed is Ritalin, which stimulates the release of neurotransmitters. There seems to be an immediate response to Ritalin once the correct dosage has been found. Children seem to become more focused, less impulsive and moody. The side effects of Ritalin can be loss of appetite and sometimes a slow down in growth for a while. Doctors can counteract these factors with a stoppage of the drug periodically at appropriate times, like vacations.

Dexadrine

Dexadrine works in a different way to achieve the same effect. Some of the side effects are more pronounced than ritalin, like moodiness and a drowsy, sedated state.

Cyclert

This has a similar effect as the other two drugs, but no one yet knows how it works. It seems to be less effective than the others and can cause and exacerbate moodiness.

Antidepressants:

Antidepressants have been found to have a similar effect to stimulants. The two most widely used are *tofranil* and *norpramin*. Side effects seem to be less severe than with stimulants, but blood pressure is monitored carefully. The difference is that children build up a tolerance to these medicines.

Your main responsibility is to make sure that proper assessment is made of your child before administering medication. It should be noted that the drugs used, especially in low doses for children, are nonaddictive and considered safe.

The question of whether to administer medication was a real problem for concerned parents Kelly and Paul. They were completely opposed to medication, especially for their child. But life was hell with seven-year-old Jamie. The entire family was turned upside-down with Jamie's hyperactivity, angry moods, troubles in school, and anti-social behavior. They tried everything, read every book, and worked at being model parents. Jamie was miserable. He was out of control, and he couldn't help himself. His self-esteem was very low, and he was becoming more and more anxious.

Finally, Jamie's pediatrician convinced Kelly and Paul to have him tested. As suspected, he did have ADHD. After much soul-searching and advice, Jamie's parents agreed to put him on Ritalin.

At first, Jamie was on too strong a dose, and he walked around in a groggy state. But by adjusting the dose and finding out the best times to give him his medication, Jamie responded wonderfully.

His life turned around. He was able to concentrate in school, other kids found him more approachable, and his parents were able to form a better relationship with him.

If parents continue to live in denial, the child suffers the most. If you really want to help your child, get him tested before age six. Remember, ADD and ADHD is not a diagnosis for failure. With proper diagnosis, treatment, and a positive attitude, an ADD child can lead a highly successful and productive life.

WHAT TO TELL YOUR CHILD

The hardest part of I.Q. or psychological testing is how to communicate to your child what it is he will be doing.

For children under seven, it's probably best to say that you are going to play some games with Mrs. Smith. If your child is older, you can be more direct. Tell him that you are taking him to see a person who is going to see how he thinks about things, a person who wants to help him focus better on his school work.

Frame the session in a positive way, but don't say you are going to be tested to see how smart you are. Test results are not important for your child to know. You never want to create a mind-set where your child feels that he is not meeting a certain standard set for him.

Knowing his score or I.Q. can work in negative ways. If

the score is high, and your child is not working up to his potential because of various problems (focus, ADD, learning disabilities), then she could be continually frustrated. If the score is low, your child might perceive herself as "stupid" and not even try to work up to her potential.

Giftedness does not insure success, and low test scores do not mean one is destined to failure. The child may simply not test well. Many factors can influence the testing process: a child's health, mentally and physically; attention problems; and the fact that your child may be resistant to any sort of testing, given his particular learning style.

For this reason, Dr. Schulman feels every child should be given an I.Q. test and placed on an early learning curve, then retested as the years progress. Christie was so adamant that her daughter be placed in a gifted program that the school finally agreed even though Allison did not test as gifted. Christie was sure that the testing process was wrong. Allison struggled in the program, and Christie was disappointed in her performance. Allison's school work was not only suffering, but her self-esteem was very low. Finally, she begged to go back to her regular classes and ended up doing extremely well.

This story points out that it is not important that your child perceive herself as gifted or ADD or challenging or anything else. What's important is that the child feel good about herself. That is the recipe for success.

GIFTED CHALLENGERS

Gifted children can pose a double challenge for parents. First, you may be trying to deal with the problems of a challenging child or a one with ADD. Then, if you are faced with the possibility that your child is gifted, a whole new set of circumstances arises.

Giftedness is about how a child thinks—how he generalizes, connects ideas, and finds alternative solutions. The knowledge of facts about a particular subject will not create a gifted child. It's his own thoughts and ideas about that subject that display giftedness. Gifted kids analyze, invent, and constantly create new ways to approach learning. They don't always get the highest grades in class. In fact, many gifted challengers are developmentally immature.

This is shown in the case of 10-year-old Michael. Michael sat in class, disruptive, constantly trying to get attention, always questioning and demanding. Instead of being recommended for a gifted program, he was shoved aside as a problem child who "probably" had attention deficit problems. His schoolwork did not reflect giftedness, but his teacher did not know what to really look for.

Subsequently, Michael was found to have ADHD. But he was also gifted. This was not detected until years later by a sensitive and knowing teacher who recommended that he be retested for the gifted program.

Parents should become educated about their child's special needs and gifts. Even if a youngster is gifted without the other complexities, this presents many challenges in itself. The following is only a partial list of gifted traits and how these traits can sometimes impact in a negative way:

Gifted Traits

- **Intense curiosity** Demanding, asking questions, won't leave you alone. These kids can be very exhausting.
- **Perfectionists** Afraid to do anything because they are afraid to fail. They may jump in and not let go or may be impatient of others. Perfectionism runs in families. Parents need to watch their own behavior and accept their mistakes.
- **Loners** May have a hard time collaborating and end up being loners because they feel superior to their group.
- **Boredom** Need to be stimulated. They can irritate a teacher by challenging information the teacher gives, and the teacher can get angry. The child demands more work from the teacher, and she may not be prepared to meet the child's needs.
- **Quick-to-learn** Learn on first pass. They usually don't need repetition. Teachers are often at a loss to keep these kids stimulated.
- **Sensitive** High degree of sensitivity. Gifted children are open and get their feelings hurt easily. This is a defining characteristic of a gifted child.
- **Nonconformists** Creates original ideas, sometimes rebellious.
- **Long attention span** Difficult to get these kids away from what they're working on.
- **Convergent thinkers** Have the ability to bring several ideas together to create a cohesive whole.
- **Divergent thinkers** Have the ability to create many ideas and are excellent during brainstorming sessions, but can be distracted by the next idea.

ADD kids conversely would have a short attention span. Nevertheless, they still can be gifted.

SOCIAL ISSUES FOR GIFTED CHALLENGERS

Highly gifted kids have trouble finding friends that they can relate to. They may engage in complex pursuits that other children might not understand.

It's necessary for your child to be with kids who stimulate her. Seek enriching environments like camps, computer programs, art museum programs, and sports where your child comes into contact with other kids with similar interests and abilities.

All of these issues for gifted kids are compounded with an ADD challenging child. A gifted ADHD child has even more problems because he is often so disruptive that other children avoid him.

Putting your child in a school where there are other children like himself will make him feel like he belongs.

FINDING THE RIGHT SCHOOL

You need to find an environment that's conducive to helping your child. Gifted kids need to move ahead at their own pace. A more open structure encourages kids to take responsibility for their weekly work and progress independently. But a gifted ADD child might do better in a structured environment. The open structure could be too distracting for an unfocused child.

The balance between meeting gifted needs and providing enriching materials, but at the same time creating an overall structure, optimally serves a gifted and challenging child.

Schools will make accommodations for learning disabilities. For instance, one young teen who was ADD and gifted was allowed to take the S.A.T. in a room all by herself without a time limit.

Some children may be entitled to tutors and readers (someone who will read the material on tape for them) if they have ADD or learning disabilities.

ALLERGIES AND OTHER FACTORS

Although the verdict is unclear, food allergies may contribute to challenging behavior. Some parents report that their children do better when food allergies are addressed. For example, four-year-old Traci went to a birthday party and ate chocolate cake, chocolate candy, and chocolate milk. When she came home, she was "bouncing off the walls." Her mother described her as rolling around on the carpet almost uncontrollably. She jumped and ran around the house for hours.

Laura thought something was terribly wrong. Traci had many more of these episodes, and Laura thought her little girl was becoming more and more difficult.

Every morning, Traci had chocolate milk for breakfast and chocolate cookies in the afternoon. A clear pattern emerged, but not until Laura took Traci to a psychologist who had the foresight to recommend that she be tested for food allergies.

As you can imagine, Traci did have a sensitivity to chocolate. The caffeine and sugar alone gave her such a "rush" that she couldn't contain her behavior. Once she was taken off of chocolate and sugar, her behavior changed drastically. She was calm and focused.

Watch your child's behavior after he eats foods like chocolate. You may want to cut down on sugary sweets and colas. Caffeine is a powerful stimulant and shouldn't be given unless a doctor suggests it.

If you suspect that your child might have a food allergy, then get him tested. You might discover that your challenging child isn't so challenging after all.

Turn to your pediatrician for guidance. Tell her your fears and ask for referrals for trained individuals in the various areas of attention deficit and giftedness.

Don't be afraid to see more than one person if you are not satisfied with just one professional's advice, especially if a doctor has recommended medication. Be open to testing procedures, and don't evaluate one test score as the extent of your child's abilities or limitations.

Look to outside organizations for help and support. Your pediatrician, child psychologist, or educational tester can give you a list of groups.

8

Parents Talk About Their Challengers

QUESTIONS AND ANSWERS

Q. My daughter loses her temper over "nothing" and then has trouble getting under control. How can I handle this?

A. Challengers escalate easily. The first thing to do is to examine what "nothing" is. It is important to find out what triggered the tantrum, after you have said in a sing-song, broken-record fashion, "When you're done crying or screaming we can talk about what happened." The issue is to avoid power struggles by removing yourself from the situation. The more you respond to the tantrum, the more reinforcing it is. Therefore, your attention prolongs the tantrum. The important point is that you are willing to talk about the problem only when your child is under control.

Q. My nine-year-old son will not take "no" for an answer. Help!

A. The best way to deal with not taking "no" for an answer is to look first at whether you have given in to your child's pleadings or beggings in the past. This becomes very reinforcing behavior in the sense that children won't believe your "no" if you have given in before. The inability to say "no" is often triggered by a parent's desire to be liked or to be seen as a good parent. Giving in has the opposite effect in that your challenger will make more and more requests leaving you even more frustrated. See Chapter 3 on discipline to help you with this issue. Check out the section on the 4 Cs.

Q. Is four years old too young to talk about "feelings" with a child?

A. No. At birth children are emotionally mature. This is especially true for challengers. They are often labeled "sensitive" children. Moreover, all children develop language in order to communicate their feelings. The more you talk about your feelings with words—rather than yelling or losing control—the better your challenger will be at doing the same. You can use puppets or stuffed animals to help challengers express their feelings in words.

Q. My daughter is called "wild" at school because she likes to play rough with the boys and gets rambunctious. Should I tame her spirit?

A. No. Your challenger is not "wild." She probably has a high degree of kinesthetic ability. This goes back to the seven different types of intelligence discussed in Chapter 2. Her energy should be developed and encouraged. Moreover, avoid any labeling and stereotyping because these monikers adversely affect self-esteem. Channel her energy into sports or other physical activities. Challengers need to be understood as unique and encouraged to develop the skills they already possess—perhaps through coaching or team sports.

Q. Is it better for a challenging child to be in a structured or unstructured school environment? Why?

A. Challengers need both structured and unstructured school experiences. The degree of structure depends on the individual needs of your child. In a classroom setting, challengers need clear limits and expectations by teachers. In terms of classroom management, a teacher should provide clear behavioral expectations coupled with plenty of positive reinforcement. However, because challengers often have varied learning styles that do not fit easily into a typical classroom, parents may need to educate their school about their challenger's learning style and find appropriate ways to meet their child's needs. Please refer to the section on the seven different learning styles for a detailed discussion of this issue.

Q. My seven-year-old son is so defiant. I say "up." He says "down." I say "no." He says "yes." How do I handle this behavior?

A. Challengers often have difficulty with transitions. Preparing your child in advance may help alleviate the "pushing and pulling." The best way to prepare challengers is by clarifying your expectation before the situation occurs. This helps to avoid power struggles. For example, if your son balks at bedtime then it is important to use the 4 Cs prior to bedtime so that he knows that unless he goes to bed when asked that there will be a consequence that you will *consistently* follow through with. Unless you are willing to set clear, reasonable expectations, your challenger won't understand that you say what you mean, and mean what you say! See Chapter 3 on discipline.

Q. I give and give—love, attention, caring, material objects—to my nine-year-old daughter, but it never seems to be enough. I'm fed up. What can I do?

A. Challengers sometimes appear insatiable. It seems as though whatever you do is never enough. In my experience, challengers become demanding when they are feeling anxious. What they are anxious about varies from situation to situation. For example, in planning a birthday party, one challenger had trouble limiting the number of friends invited because she was afraid of alienating anyone left off the list. In this situation she needed reassurance and support that although some classmates might feel left out, she has remained friends with kids who did not invite her to their parties.

Q. My seven-year-old son never seems to listen. I tell him to do something and it's like talking to a wall. What can I do?

A. Challengers often have difficulty listening. They usually pay attention; however, they are easily distracted. In Chapter 3 we talk about ways to help your child listen. For example, it's important to get down to your son's level, make eye contact, speak in a natural voice, and say to your son in his own words what you have requested. Sometimes parents overload their challengers with requests. It's better to ask for one or two things at a time. Be sure to praise your son's work once he's completed the tasks before making any other requests.

Q. My family background was filled with anger, fights, and a totally dysfunctional household. I'm worried this will impact my six-year-old daughter as I see already that I lose my temper and get angry over small things when I'm tense. How can I avoid a repeat of my lousy childhood?

A. You already are taking the first step by recognizing that behaviors you learned as a child in your own family directly impact the way you discipline and react to your daughter. Challengers require us to establish clear guidelines and expectations of behavior from them. When there are clear limits with appropriate consequences, family conflict and escalating outbursts are alleviated. Parents of challengers are especially prone to reenacting the past because of the constant demands challengers present. They understand that when they overreact, it only reinforces their child's own escalation. Parents sometimes need time-out as much as challengers. Fair family meetings are a good way to share feelings and reduce tensions by finding appropriate ways to resolve conflicts.

Q. I find my challenging 11-year-old daughter says things that are hurtful like, "I can't stand this family." I know she doesn't mean it, but it disturbs me. Am I being too sensitive?

A. It's normal for children to express in hurtful ways their anger or disappointment with things that happen in the family. Again if you are concerned, this issue can make a very productive topic for a fair family meeting. Follow the guidelines established in Chapter 2 before you start. You might start with the question "How can we make the family work together better?"

Q. My husband often asks our son, "What's wrong with you? Why can't you concentrate? Why can't you be better?" I don't think my son can. Will my husband's comments hurt him?

A. There is a lot of research that indicates that sons who are criticized by their fathers have diminished self-esteem, lower academic achievement, poor social relationships, and difficulties in their sex-role identification (their ability to understand how boys are supposed to act with friends, family, or at school). This issue of concentration is not something that should be a subject of criticism. In fact, lack of concentration may indicate distractibility which, coupled with other problems, may indicate a learning disability or attention deficit disorder. These problems need to be addressed. The help of a learning specialist or educational psychologist is appropriate. Educational testing may be required.

Q. My daughter always wants to be first. She'll even cheat or push her way to be first. I've discussed this with her many times and given her the "winning isn't everything" talk, but it doesn't seem to help. What do you suggest?

A. Parents sometimes inadvertently convey the message that *being* the best is more important than *doing* your best. Challengers may pick up your unconscious message that succeeding is more important than trying. Parents need to examine their own responses to losing a tennis match or not winning at Scrabble. Challengers sometimes hope that by winning they will feel less anxious about not being able to do things other kids can do. For example, some challengers want to be first in line to kick the soccer ball because the anticipatory anxiety of having to wait makes them so anxious that they will make a mistake or fail in some way. The waiting makes them anxious, and their anxiety diminishes their performance.

Q. My son is so difficult. He fits the challenger profile perfectly. Will it ever change. I'm a quiet, mild-mannered mom, and I'm lost.

A. Challengers *are* difficult. They often see the world differently from you. Nevertheless, your son needs the qualities that you offer in order to learn and relate to others. Entering your child's world requires you define the areas of difficulty. Specifically, decide which issue is the most important to address. Utilize some of the skills discussed in Chapter 4 on problem-solving techniques as a starting point.

Q. Aren't all toddlers challenging, especially little boys? Mine is so active, strong-willed, and oppositional. Will he grow out of this?

A. Of course toddlers can be challenging. Often it makes little difference whether your toddler is a boy or a girl. Toddler boys may have difficulty "winding down" because they tend to be physically active and have high energy levels. This presents a unique challenge for parents to find the appropriate balance between encouraging their son's independence while establishing appropriate limits. The important point is that once toddlers become overstimulated or overtired they are more likely to escalate emotionally and appear strong-willed. By utilizing the 4 Cs outlined in Chapter 3 you will be able to establish better limits that reduce the likelihood of oppositional behavior or tantrums.

Q. I've said some terrible things to my eight-year-old in a fit of frustration. Even though I've apologized, will this scar her for life?

A. I believe that it is important to apologize to our children when we have made a mistake. Rarely does one event or one type of interaction scar a child for life. Nevertheless, to reduce the long-term impact of our mistakes, we must not only apologize but also make the appropriate behavioral changes in order for our children—especially challengers—to believe what we say. This also teaches our challengers that change is possible and that we can learn from our mistakes. In our relationships with our children we are not looking for perfection, but rather a willingness to make corrections. Hopefully, that willingness to correct our mistakes minimizes the wounds that we may have caused.

Q. My daughter and her fourth grade teacher are in constant conflict. What can I do to help?

A. Your first approach is to call a parent/teacher conference. Prior to the conference, establish specifically what the areas of conflict are. If your child presents unique challenges, be sure to describe them and make recommendations to the teacher about ways or methods that have worked in previous classes. Indicate your willingness to implement at home any of the teacher's appropriate suggestions. If the problem centers on differences between your child's learning style and the teacher's teaching style, then the discussion should include the school counselor or principal. This type of conflict sometimes warrants changing the teacher. However, this change should only be done if a better match is achieved between your challenger's learning style and another teacher's teaching style.

Q. I set limits and boundaries, but my 11-year-old son keeps pushing me. I feel like I'm always taking privileges away. Any other suggestions?

A. First, you are not taking away privileges. Your son's actions lead to the privileges being taken away. The purpose of setting limits is to teach your son to take responsibility for his behavior. However, an alternative might be to have a fair family meeting to discuss how your son can succeed. For example, if your son regularly forgets to remove his games from the hall, and the consequence is that the games left are taken away for a day, then in a fair family meeting the discussion might focus on how you can help your son keep more of his games. Perhaps, he has ideas that would help or perhaps he needs a different type of reminder—like a sign on his bedroom door saying, "Don't forget the hall!"

Q. How do you make demanding kids realize that parents have things to do also? They don't get it.

A. All children are demanding. They want what they want when they want it. Challengers often escalate their demands to such a degree that it appears that they are impossible to satisfy. Helping challengers tolerate unsatisfied desires requires parents to follow two steps: First, parents must prepare their challenger by agreeing upon what is a reasonable demand. As part of this first step you must validate your child's feelings. For example, if you take your daughter to the supermarket, then let her know that you understand that she would like to choose five cereals, but she can only choose two. Second, you must explain that if she complains or demands more than what was agreed upon, then there will be consequences—like leaving the market and the shopping cart behind while she is given a time-out in the car. You can decide to give her another chance; however, a clear consequence must be stated before you return to the market. For example, you might say, "I'm willing to give you another chance; however, if the same thing happens, we will leave the store completely and not return today."

Q. My six-year-old daughter and I seem to argue over everything—the clothes she wears mostly. What should I emphasize and what should I let go?

A. As you rightly indicate, it is important to pick your fights. Otherwise, everything becomes a battle. As an organizing principle, limits are important around safety and health-related issues. For example, if your daughter wanted to go outside barefoot on a snowy day, setting a limit that she must wear protective shoes is appropriate. The color of the shoes or how many socks she wears would be irrelevant. Challengers, in particular, may have sensitivities to certain fabrics and chemicals that make it more difficult to choose what to wear. In power struggles, no one wins. The bad feelings generated over which dress to wear or what color shoes is appropriate lasts far longer than the situation. Often children need to learn from natural consequences—as long as the situations aren't dangerous. For example, if your daughter wants to wear her jeans to a dressy birthday party, then seeing the other kids' reactions to what she's worn will teach her an important lesson and is a natural consequence to her actions and choices.

Q. My son's personality escalates, and he gives into tantrums when he is tired, but when I try to get him to sleep early, he fights me every inch of the way. What should I do?

A. It's important to establish sleep rituals that actually serve as a time for winding down. Playing Nintendo or watching action movies prior to bedtime does not promote rest. One suggestion is to plan quiet time about an hour before bedtime. For example, preparing for bedtime by your son cleaning his room, then brushing his teeth, then listening to familiar music followed by reading a story is the type of ritual that promotes sleep. Moreover, rituals take time before they become habits. Be consistent for several days before making any adjustments in your plan. If you make changes, be sure they meet the test of increasing quiet time.

9

The Long Road Home

As you have discovered by the end of this book, there are no easy answers. Parenting a challenging child takes an enormous amount of education, effort, patience, and understanding.

We ask you to explore not only your child's psychological world, but your own as well. Good parenting skills are not just about finding out what's wrong with your child. Parenting involves your participation in helping your child interact with his family, school, and friends.

Nothing has more of an impact for parents than a moment of clarity—when that light goes on in their heads and they say, "I finally understand why my child acts this way." This enlightenment can change the course of your child's life—and yours.

Understanding only occurs with a desire to change and to be open to hearing some things that you may not want to. The patterns of negative behavior that we establish as children will stay with us for the rest of our lives, unless we address them. If your parents yelled at you and criticized you all the time, then chances are, unless you consciously want to change that pattern, you will yell at and criticize *your* child. Parents usually model what was modeled to them.

By reading this book, you have made a choice to change. Right now, go to your child and say, "I have just read a book about how we can work together better. I know we have had some problems, but I love you, and I want you to feel good about yourself." *Talking* to your child is the first step toward understanding; *listening* is the next.

What your child says might surprise you. Parents do so much talking "at" their child that parenting becomes a one-way line of communication.

By engaging your child in family meetings, you might get a clue to your challenger's social world, his view of school, and what interests him. Entering your child's world will clearly help you to understand him better and to make better choices and decisions as his parent.

PARENT AUTHOR'S EPILOGUE

Recently, I entered my own daughter's world. I volunteered to work in her second grade class. I watched my Alexandra fidget and fuss, half-listening to the teacher. She kept throwing me kisses, looking around the room, and every once in a while, she raised her hand in excited earnest to answer a question she really hadn't a clue about.

I watched her with interest, with concern, and with sudden rapt fascination. After about 15 minutes, I realized I was no longer seeing my challenging daughter. I was seeing a reflection of myself in the second grade—the same little girl—fidgeting and talking and half-listening to the teacher.

I had worked so hard to change Alexandra, to get her to conform to a set of standards that I thought was appropriate. But in reality it was neither appropriate for her or for me.

It occurred to me after many, many months of writing this book that Alexandra is still not, and probably never will be, your "primary color kind of kid." When I began writing *The Challenging Child,* I thought that this miraculous change would take place in my daughter when I uncovered everything about her that I had yet to understand. She would no longer be a challenge. But the irony is that most of the change that has taken place during this year has been in me.

The real discovery came when I was writing Chapter 2 on the parents' challenge. Some very stark realizations about my own behavior became clear. I realized that by trying to change my daughter's nature, I was trying to alter the very human being I loved so dearly. This was not only impossible, it was detrimental to her sense of self. I got angry with Alexandra just for being who she was. Yes, at times I longed for her to be more sensitive, more demonstrative, less argumentative. She would express an opinion, and I couldn't accept it because I had a preconditioned attitude about "right" and "wrong" ideas. I often found her behavior—manipulative, oppositional, and pushy—intolerable.

Did I want her to be a different child or a better-behaved version of the child she was? Then I realized that this was the paradox. The child she was would always possess some of the traits I didn't like. The challenge was how I, as the parent, perceived and reacted to these traits.

By exploring our different learning styles, I was able to understand how she approached life—school, social situations, sports, and creative endeavors. I was also able to temper my own parental behaviors, especially my need to overcontrol and restrict her choices. I learned to let go and allow her to express herself in the way that she felt most comfortable.

The change was not quick. Often we slipped back into "challenging hell" and it seemed like every trait converged on me at once.

But as we have emphasized over and over in the book, you must be *consistent* and *persistent*. Follow the Parent Plans, and most importantly look at your own motivations and what kind of an impact your behavior has on your child.

Without a doubt, challengers are the exciting adults of the future. If channeled correctly, all of their traits can serve them in a positive way. After all, any child can use primary colors, but think of what a child who chases magenta madness and serpent scale green can accomplish!